BAIRD SEARLES

EPIC!
HISTORY ON THE BIG SCREEN

Harry N. Abrams, Inc. • Publishers • New York

This book is dedicated to
all the four-footed actors
(especially the horses),
some of whom suffered and even died
in the making of these films
which would have been so much the less
without their beauty and grace.

Editor: Beverly Fazio
Designers: Judith Michael and Jody Hanson
Photo Editor: John K. Crowley

Library of Congress Cataloging-in-Publication Data

Searles, Baird.
    EPIC! : history on the big screen / by Baird Searles.
        p.   cm.
    Includes bibliographical references.
    Filmography: p. 231
    ISBN 0–8109–3402–7
    1. Historical films—History and criticism. 2. Motion pictures—History. I. Title.
PN1995.9.H5S4   1990
791.43′658—dc20   90–32341
                                                                                    CIP

Endpapers: *Ben-Hur* (1959): And they're rounding the first turn. . . .
The figures on the *spina* are most colossal in this, the second film version of a novel by Lew Wallace.

Pages 2–3: *The Clan of the Cave Bear:* The movie was a brave, if not totally successful, attempt to picture mankind's life before history began.

Text copyright © 1990 Baird Searles
Illustrations copyright © 1990 Harry N. Abrams, Inc.
Film copyrights on page 240

Published in 1990 by Harry N. Abrams, Incorporated, New York
A Times Mirror Company

Printed and bound in Japan

CONTENTS

FOREWORD

When the monumental works of man are cited, they are often the Pyramids or the Great Wall of China, or, of the more interchangeable modern efforts, one of the huge dams or tall buildings of this century. Seldom if ever, when such things come up, does one hear any mention of the movies. And yet, if one looks at what went into the colossal spectacles produced for the cinema, the sheer amount of money, energy, material, manpower, and persons involved could manage to challenge the greatest of more substantial endeavors. That the end result of this was a few round cans filled with film seems outré, logical, and very much of the modern age.

Most of these films were retellings of history. Much has been made of the laughable inaccuracy of cinematic re-creations of the past. And certainly that was justified in a way (though some of the later examples are miracles of research and veracity). But if the films are considered as dramas rather than documentaries, poetic license is surely allowed in production as well as story, in dialogue as well as characters. (As we shall see, Shakespeare's histories were hardly textbook examples of reality.) In that light, many of the great historical spectaculars were ludicrous, many were enthralling. Many were both. And much of the world's population knows what little it knows of history from these movies. What follows is a study of themes and variations, with history (as much of it as we know) as the theme, and the movies as beautiful, stirring, spectacular, and/or comic variations.

The Ten Commandments (1956): The high point of the last of the great DeMille epics was the depiction of the Exodus.

ANTIQUITY

EUROPE—PREHISTORY

The misty beginnings of human civilization, despite a good deal of publicity, are still remarkably unclear. In the past several decades, anthropological discoveries have certainly opened new areas of knowledge and have equally opened endless amounts of disagreement among the experts. The details of human life before written history begins are still almost entirely speculative, and all that has been written or pictured of that life has, at best, relied on shrewd guesswork from remarkably little physical evidence. At worst, there has been endless nonsense about the life of the "cave man."

The cinema has been one of the worst perpetrators of this kind of misinformation, pitting cave men—or, more usually, cave women in the briefest of bearskins—against ravening dinosaurs in epics of anthropological inaccuracy (not that some of these weren't in the best tradition of imaginative moviemaking). But it was relatively late in film history that any attempt at realism was made in depicting the Stone Age on the silver screen.

The first major attempt at primeval *verismo* was *Quest For Fire* (1981), set in Europe some 80,000 years ago, when there was a number of species of primitive man, the best known of which was the Neanderthal. The movie concerns one tribe of hunters whose major cultural asset seems to be the use of fire. An attack on their cave by an even more primitive group leads to their flight to a marshy island and the loss of their fire, which they have no idea how to rekindle.

Three of the males embark on an epic trek to find fire. They finally succeed in stealing it from a cannibal tribe, at the same time liberating a female captive for whom the leader of the three, Naoh, conceives an attachment. She is from a higher culture group with whom they have a brief sojourn before returning with the fire to their own people.

In the hullabaloo of their return, the fire is lost in the water, but from his

Salome (1918): We assume that Salome was a blasé lady, but Theda Bara seems to take it too far. Presumably those are some of the seven veils scattered about her person and the set.

mate's people Naoh has learned how to make fire. Friction triumphantly saves the day.

The film is, de facto, primitive. There is no witty dialogue (no comprehensible dialogue at all, in fact), no great psychological insights, no subtlety. The plot proceeds by incident; these vary from the sexual to the silly (the three mighty hunters being treed for days by even mightier lions). But there are moments of great beauty—the tiny isolated figures against the vast, empty landscapes—and high drama, such as an encounter with a herd of mammoth. The scene is vibrant with imminent danger and is dominated by close-ups of the infinitely wary, infinitely wise eye of the herd leader. The resolution of the scene, the acceptance of each species by the other, leaves the viewer limp. The four major actors (Everett McGill, Ron Perlman, Nameer el-Kadi, and Rae Dawn Chong) superbly master the difficulties of acting and appearing to be what are in effect members of a race unknown to today's world.

Despite an inapropros score (one of those Scriabinesque choral numbers that screams "Epic!") and an emphasis on primitive sexuality that verges on the exploitative, *Quest For Fire* is a brilliant evocation of a time when man himself was an endangered species.

The next big attempt at depicting the picturesquely primitive was the filming of Jean M. Auel's *The Clan of the Cave Bear* (1986), and it came a cropper. The period was the Wurm glaciation of the late Pleistocene about 35,000 years ago, a relatively brief period when the Neanderthal and our kind of people (the Cro-Magnon) co-existed. Though handsomely filmed, the movie attempted too many sophisticated concepts, and where it wasn't incoherent it was almost hilariously anachronistic in its view of women's rights and race relations.

Sodom and Gomorrah: The moviemakers' idea of high life in Sodom.

CANAAN—20TH CENTURY B.C.

The Middle East was as much a simmering stew in the twentieth century before Christ as it is in the twentieth century after. Then as now, myriad races and cultures were jockeying for power, led by the Sumerian city-states.

Abram of Sumerian Ur left that city, possibly because of political troubles, possibly because of trade potential elsewhere, and with his extended family traversed the Fertile Crescent to the shores of the Mediterranean, to the country called Canaan. The stock of the nomadic clan had now grown so extensive that Abram's nephew Lot and his immediate family separated and went toward the five "Cities of the Plain" near the Dead Sea (the best known of which were Sodom and Gomorrah), which, according to the Bible, were so wantonly wicked that four of them were destroyed by a rain of fire. No trace of these cities has been found, but it has been speculated that they lie beneath the shallower portion of the Dead Sea.

Sodom and Gomorrah: The wicked "Cities of the Plain" are destroyed by the special effects technicians.

One suspects that *Sodom and Gomorrah* (1962) was made simply to cash in on a titillating title. The two wicked cities were pretty tame by contemporary standards, though the beautiful Anouk Aimée did her best to look decadent as Queen Bera of Sodom (or maybe Gomorrah), even while delivering lines such as, "Greetings, Sodomites and Israelites!" The stalwart Stewart Granger struggled mightily as Lot, who with his family, including Sodomite wife Pier Angeli, became involved in the Plain Cities' sexual and political intrigues.

The final destruction of the cities was carried off with some effectiveness; the interpretation of "rain of fire" as an implied mushroom cloud, however, pushed the contemporary relevance a bit hard. But the real audience-pleaser was the salinization of Lot's wife, who *would* look back against orders. Lot's subsequent incest with his daughters was delicately ignored by the script.

EGYPT—14TH CENTURY B.C.

Akhenaton, pharaoh of the 18th Dynasty of Egypt, has been called the first individual in history. Revolting against the already ages-old religion and culture of his country, he attempted to establish the worship of a single new god, Aton. We know a surprising amount about his family: his mother, the old Queen Tiy, born a commoner; his sister, Baketamon; his wife, the beautiful Nefertiti; and his six daughters, one of whom was married to a young princeling named Tutankhamen.

Akhenaton's stubborn commitment to change brought chaos to the country, ruin to the vast empire conquered by his father, and an end to the dynasty, which concluded with the short-lived Tutankhamen and the usurping general, Horemheb.

The Egyptian (1954), from the novel by Mika Waltari, is one of the finest of historical spectaculars, combining a production as lavish as any that had come before with a script containing a certain amount of depth and resonance. In it the rule of Akhenaton is viewed through the eyes of the young physician, Sinuhe (Edmund Purdom), who with his schoolmate, Horemheb (Victor Mature) enters the service of the newly crowned pharaoh (Michael Wilding).

Sinuhe is hardly the usual brawny hero of epic. Naive and questioning, he is brought to ruin and disgrace through his infatuation with the Babylonian courtesan Nefer and must flee the country. When he returns, Egypt is on the brink of collapse due to Akhenaton's reforms, and Horemheb enlists his aid in poisoning Pharaoh, hoping to gain the throne through marriage to Princess Baketamon (Gene Tierney).

There are no great set-piece production scenes in the movie, but images stay in the mind: the white-robed, flower-crowned followers of Aton in their temple open to the sky; Akhenaton and Nefertiti holding court, interrupted by one of their daughters; the stews and alleys of the Egyptian poor; Nefer's bawdy house, with dancers straight from tomb paintings. The art direction is lavish but amazingly authentic, down to the blue faience jars of Sinuhe's physician's kit.

Characters come alive, also. There is Judith Evelyn as the vulgar, beer-swilling Queen Mother, and Gene Tierney turns in a striking performance as the iron-willed, ambitious princess. Jean Simmons, as Merit, the tavern maid who loves Sinuhe, is so astonishingly beautiful that her strong performance of a potentially insipid role is almost eclipsed; and Peter Ustinov nearly steals the picture as the servant Kaptah.

Add an atmospheric score by Alfred Newman and Bernard Herrman featuring the sound of the Egyptian sistrum and a choral setting of the *Hymn To the Sun* written by Akhenaton himself, and you have in all an epic film of surprising substance.

The Egyptian: Sinuhe (Edmund Purdom) arrives too late to save Merit (Jean Simmons), as the followers of Akhenaton and his god are slaughtered by the forces of Horemheb (Victor Mature, right).

EGYPT/SINAI—13TH CENTURY B.C.

The descendants of Abraham had come to Egypt through Joseph and his brothers, and had lived there for centuries, through the reign of Akhenaton and the end of the 18th Dynasty. Though no Egyptian records make note of the events of Exodus, it is certain that sometime during the thirteenth century B.C., Hebrews broke free from an increasingly harsh rule by the Egyptians and fled under a charismatic leader named Moses, wandered in Sinai for many years as nomads, and eventually conquered the land of Canaan. Most evidence leads to the conclusion that the Pharaoh of the Oppression was either the great builder, Sethos I, or his successor, Rameses II, a grandiose and tyrannical ruler if ever there was one. It then follows that either Rameses or his successor, the weaker Merneptah, was the Pharaoh of the Exodus. The thirteenth century B.C. began a time of restlessness and strife in the eastern Mediterranean which was to continue into the next century, as we shall see. During Merneptah's reign, there was an invasion of Egypt by the "Peoples of the Sea," barbarians from Greece. Under the circumstances, a runaway band of slave workers was the least of Pharaoh's problems. There's no evidence that any Pharaoh drowned in the Red Sea.

Overleaf:

The Egyptian: Gene Tierney turned in a powerful performance as Akhenaton's ambitious sister, the Princess Baketamon. The Egyptian settings were magnificent and more authentic than most.

13

Opposite:
The Ten Commandments (1923): A good time is had by all as Estelle Taylor leads the wandering tribes of Israel in the worship of the Golden Calf.

The Ten Commandments (1923): The monumental set for the gates of Pharaoh's city, first time around.

The Ten Commandments (1956): An obelisk is dragged into place by Pharaoh's Jewish slaves.

The Ten Commandments (1956): The monumental set for the gates of Pharaoh's city, second time around.

Samson and Delilah: Delilah (Hedy Lamarr) turns over the barbered Samson (Victor Mature) to the Philistine general (the enduring Henry Wilcoxon).

Opposite:

Samson and Delilah: Tresses regrown, Samson demolishes the premises, starting with some pillars that don't look all that stable to begin with.

When Cecil B. DeMille first filmed *The Ten Commandments* in 1923, less than half the movie was devoted to the biblical story; the rest was a modern morality tale. In the biblical section, we were shown the Exodus, the parting of the Red Sea, and the worship of the Golden Calf, brought to a halt with the introduction of the tablets of the law. It was, in effect, a collection of moving biblical illustrations. The Red Sea sequence was a rouser, with howling winds, towering walls of water, and Pharaoh's army swept away. True to form, in the midst of all this, DeMille includes an artful shot of three lissome Hebrew maidens perched decoratively on a rock, with draperies blowing in the wind and suitable expressions of awe and fear.

More than thirty years later, DeMille decided to rework the subject to take advantage of the vogue for epics brought on by the advent of the wide screen. And advantage was certainly taken. The result was a full-scale biography of Moses, all wool and hundreds of yards wide, the epitome of the gaudy, pious, lowbrow spectacle. Charlton Heston was Moses, dashing as a youthful "Egyptian" prince, scruffy as a fugitive Israelite, Michelangelically massive as a patriarch. DeMille's scriptwriters have settled on Sethos I (here Sethi) as the Pharaoh of the Oppression; Sir Cedric Hardwicke is appropriately old-school-dynasty in the role. Yul Brynner paces ferociously as Rameses, and manages to look strikingly ancient Egyptian. The same cannot be said for Anne Baxter, one of those ladies who appears modern no matter how authentic the costum-

ing; she plays the Princess Nefretiri, who wants to have her own Camp David Accord with Moses but settles for Rameses. Judith Anderson does a pharaonic Mrs. Danvers as the nurse who knows the secret of Moses' birth. There are several such subplots, involving the likes of Edward G. Robinson, Debra Paget, and John Derek (as Joshua). The big production numbers are the raising of an obelisk, the parting of the Red Sea (which bears a remarkable resemblance to the 1923 sequence, right down to the three ladies on the rock), and the engraving of the tablets by what appears to be an early form of laser printing.

Nevertheless, a good time is had by all, and the three-and-a-half hours plus that the movie runs have remarkably few tedious moments.

CANAAN—12TH CENTURY B.C.

The disturbances on the northern shore of the Mediterranean continued into the twelfth century B.C., probably because of the pressure of less civilized tribes pushing into the Greek peninsula. The results were legion: the invasion of Egypt by "Sea Peoples," the fall of the Hittite Empire, the war between the Greek states and a city in Asia Minor called Ilium, and the conquest of part of the coast of Canaan by a sea-going people, uncircumcised and worshipping strange gods, who became known as the Philistines. Links to Greek or Minoan culture are thought likely by scholars. The conquered Hebrews of the area mounted a sort of guerrilla campaign against the Philistines and their gods.

Cecil B. DeMille's *Samson and Delilah* (1949) just missed the wide screen, which is probably as well—the eye couldn't have taken in many more robes, drapes, donkeys, beards, feathers, jewels, murals, and flower-pot-shaped helmets. The movie is essentially a whitewash of Delilah, a nice Philistine girl who loves the Danite leader Samson. (The Philistines had conquered the southern coast of Canaan, which had been occupied by the Hebrew tribe of Dan.) Spurned, she betrays him, but when he is brought to the temple of Dagon to be made show of, she guides him to the supporting pillars of the edifice and remains as he pushes them apart, killing both of them and the cast of thousands.

Victor Mature as Samson is costumed to look as much like a rectangular slab of concrete as possible, but wields the jawbone of an ass more effectively than more loquacious actors. Hedy Lamarr simpers a lot as Delilah and bares her midriff constantly. George Sanders steals the show as the Philistine ruler, the Saran; wrapped in suavity, he brings off lines like "Delilah, what a dimpled dragon you can be" and raises a salutary cup as the gigantic statue of Dagon falls on him. Russ Tamblyn plays Samson's juvenile sidekick, Saul—there's speculation that he might someday grow up to lead the Danites.

The Philistine decor is eclectic, to say the least, a combination of Egyptian, Assyrian, and Minoan elements. The huge temple of Dagon, open to the sky and containing the monumental statue of the god with a furnace in its belly, falls down very satisfactorily indeed.

GREECE/TROY—12TH CENTURY B.C.

In the time of Rameses III, an Egyptian inscription notes that "the isles were restless." Apparently even in Egypt about 1196 B.C. there was news of war to the north; the upheavals of the previous century centering around the Greek peninsula continued. It seems certain that in that decade a tribe of Achaeans from Greece made war on a rich city near the mouth of the Hellespont called variously Ilium or Troy. Of the nine cities layered on that archaeological site, the sixth, a city of high walls and four gates dating to about that time, was destroyed by fire.

The details of that war continued in legend through the Dark Ages of Greece in the same way that the legends of Arthur survived through the Dark Ages of Europe. They were written down finally four centuries later by a poet (or poets) named Homer; we know them as The Iliad and The Odyssey. Though Homer was (were) Greek, it's the Trojans who are the most appealing characters in this grandest and oldest story of love and war. Whether the war really started because of the love of a man for a woman, history may never know for sure.

Helen of Troy (1956) certainly assumed so; it tells the story in the most blatantly romantic of terms, and on that level is vastly appealing. There's a ravishing Helen (Rossana Podesta) whose husband doesn't understand her and an impossibly handsome, blond Paris (Jacques Sernas) who simply gets carried away (emotionally) and didn't really mean to abduct the lady. Troy is visually a mixture of archaic Greek and Minoan, and when Paris seeks to introduce the lady who has come home with him, the adolescent Cassandra (Janette Scott) ringingly announces, "Her name is Death!" Sir Cedric Hardwicke is inevitably Priam; looking at Helen as the Greek fleet heaves into view, he inquires, "Is this the face that launched a thousand ships?" as though he'd never heard the line before.

The big production number is the hauling of the giant horse into the city; there is a fairly circumspect orgy around its base, and then as the last tipsy fluteplayer carries the last tipsy bacchante away, there is an ominous scraping sound within the horse's belly. . . .

The core of Euripides' *The Trojan Women* (1971) is four declamatory scenes (practically monologues) for the four major women of Troy who remain after the fall of the city. Michael Cacoyannis's film of the play brought together a staggering quartet of actresses. Katharine Hepburn was unquestionably magnificent as Queen Hecuba, but her forty-year career made it almost impossible to see her as anyone but Katharine Hepburn. The nearly always underrated Genevieve Bujold as Cassandra was a wild and scary prophetess-princess and Vanessa Redgrave a perfect Andromache, widow of Hector. Irene Papas raised the tension of the film a full step higher as the adopted Trojan woman, Helen, playing her as a tigerish survivor. The production was appropriately anything but lavish; a sacked city is not spectacular.

ISRAEL—10TH CENTURY B.C.

The continued threat and sometimes domination of the Philistines forced the Hebrew tribes into uniting under a king. The prophet Samuel anointed Saul; when later in his reign Saul fell out of favor with the religious party, Samuel anointed a young shepherd boy, David, who had entered Saul's household as a sort of musical therapist; his harping seemed to ease Saul's headaches and fits of rage. Also, according to another story, David had been the youngster who had defeated a nine-foot-tall Philistine giant.

When Saul was killed in battle along with all but one of his sons, David claimed his kingdom by right of his marriage to Saul's daughter. It is a very human figure that is recorded in the Bible, especially in his acquisition of his favorite wife, Bathsheba, which was accomplished by sending her husband, Uriah the Hittite, into harm's way in battle. (The Hittite Empire had collapsed in the chaos of the previous century, but apparently many surviving Hittite warriors served as mercenaries.) His reign was marred by the usual (for the time) dynastic struggles among his sons; Absalom killed Amnon and later rebelled and was killed in turn.

Queen of Sheba: Betty Blythe as the Queen of Sheba managed to hide most of the cast of thousands with her headdress.

Solomon, son of Bathsheba, eventually inherited the throne at David's death in 973 B.C. and made himself a major monarch and the kingdom of Israel a power in the Fertile Crescent. This was possible mainly because Egypt, to the west, and the various powers to the east (Assyria, the Hittites) were in a weakened state or broken. Throughout his reign, there was the familiar struggle between the religious party, strictly faithful to the monotheistic tradition, and the temptations of foreign pantheons brought by wealth, sophistication, and the visits of exotic aliens, such as the Queen of Sheba. (Sheba is generally agreed to have been a wealthy kingdom in the south of Arabia, where Yemen is now.) Solomon reinforced tradition by the building of a great temple, richly decorated. Nevertheless, on his death in 933 B.C., the kingdom split back into two (Israel and Judah) and Jerusalem was sacked by an Egypt of revived power; the riches of the Temple were carried off.

Betty Blythe starred as the *Queen of Sheba* in 1921, a movie attempting to rival those of DeMille. It was notable for the amount of breast shown by the star (all—through a gauze top), and the fact that the major production number was a pre–*Ben-Hur* chariot race, despite the lack of evidence that the Jews or the Shebans went in for chariot racing in a big way.

Opposite, above:
Helen of Troy: Paris (Jacques Sernas) introduces Helen (Rossana Podesta) to the family: cousin Aeneas (Ronald Lewis), sister Cassandra (Janette Scott), mother Hecuba (Nora Swinburne), and father Priam (Sir Cedric Hardwicke).

Opposite, below left:
Helen of Troy: The deadly horse is brought into Troy by a rejoicing population. Note the Minoan-influenced architecture.

Opposite, below right:
The Trojan Women: Two of the women most at odds: Hecuba (Katharine Hepburn, left) is queen of the city that Helen (Irene Papas) has destroyed.

The two mid-century attempts to make historical spectacles of the careers of the two great kings of Israel, David and Solomon, were both pretty dismal for very different reasons. *David and Bathsheba* (1951), in a desperate attempt to avoid the excesses of a DeMille epic, proceeded at a slow and stately pace and concentrated on the biblically brief story of David's acquisition of Bathsheba at the expense of her husband's life. The result was a sort of lavish love triangle picture, with a good deal of passion and guilt liberally covered in Old Testament pietism. Gregory Peck and Susan Hayward in the leads were two more examples of actors that looked entirely too modern-American to be convincing, and things went to pieces when Hayward batted her eyes at Peck and throatily asked, "Did you really kill Goliath?" (The David-Goliath bout is seen in flashback.)

Solomon and Sheba (1959), on the other hand, seemed to try to outdo DeMille in sheer silliness, and succeeded admirably. Tyrone Power, playing Solomon, died soon after filming began; Yul Brynner was substituted and earlier scenes were reshot. Since only a state visit of Sheba's queen is described in the Bible (something like Margaret Thatcher visiting George Bush), an overwrought plot was cooked up involving the seduction of Solomon by Sheba physically and spiritually (the latter with her exotic deities). Brynner, atypically wigged and bearded, attempted to look wise through it all; Gina Lollobrigida, at the height of the Italian sex-symbol period, wiggled mightily

David and Bathsheba: David seems a little dubious about the Ark of the Covenant. That's the prophet Nathan (Raymond Massey) on the left.

and took a bath in a B.C. hot tub. An outdoor picnic/orgy/religious service thrown by Sheba for Solomon is perhaps the epitome of the Las Vegas school of biblical filmmaking, but nevertheless seemed a bit tame for the thunder and lightning rained down on it by Jehovah.

King David (1985) attempted a much more serious examination of the life of David, tackling the intricacies of his family life and Hebrew politics of the time. Philosophically the movie seems to represent David as espousing an almost modern morality, pitted against the Old Testament wrath of the prophets, Samuel and Nathan. (He rebels against Nathan's order to kill all "heathens," for instance.) Samuel, in particular, is presented as shockingly bloodthirsty by contemporary Western standards; he is shown excoriating Saul for not totally eliminating the Amalekites rather than holding their king for ransom.

The film doesn't neglect the usual elements of the David story; Goliath and Bathsheba are present, the 23rd Psalm is sung to Saul, and Richard Gere as David does a spectacularly physical dance before the Ark, a subject of much derision by critics. (How did they expect David to dance—a carefully choreographed Baryshnikov-type solo?) But brought to the fore are David's complicated family relationships, with Saul's daughter Mical and with his hotheaded sons. The ambiguity of the film's morality is compounded by the

Solomon and Sheba: Solomon (Yul Brynner) and Sheba (Gina Lollobrigida) have a pastoral moment during her state visit.

Opposite:
Solomon and Sheba: The Queen of Sheba, 1959 version, was comparatively well covered.

King David: Richard Gere (left) is David. Cherie Lunghi is Michal, David's first wife and daughter to Saul, the patriarchal figure seen between them, played by Edward Woodward, TV's dapper "Equalizer."

ending. David reigns long and happily after conceding to the prophet Nathan, but on his deathbed tells his son Solomon "to follow the instincts of your heart" and to ignore the prophets.

There is an attempt to be true to the period and locale in costumes and sets; clothes are mostly homespun rather than silk robes, buildings mud brick and mortar rather than marble halls. The small rooms are constantly adrift with smoke from the burning braziers. Authenticity and a strong cast (Gere, Edward Woodward as Saul, and the talented Cherie Lunghi as Mical, much more interesting than Bathsheba), however, didn't succeed in reestablishing the Bible as a source for movie scripts.

BABYLON—9TH CENTURY B.C.

Over the next several centuries, empires rose and fell with monotonous regularity in the Fertile Crescent. One of the most fierce of these was the Assyrian, and for several years in its bloody history in the ninth century B.C., a woman ruled. She was Sammuramat, and she did a good enough job as regent to go down in legend as the mighty Semiramis, conquering queen and builder of Babylon (which had, of course, existed for centuries).

The Queen of Babylon (1956) compounded confusion by presenting an hilarious mishmash of history and legend. Rhonda Fleming, as Semiramis, is first discovered as a redheaded goatherd, perched decoratively on a rock with her pipes in hand. The plot has something to do with the Assyrians, who have just conquered Babylon, fighting the Chaldeans (a Babylonian tribe), who are not about to submit to them. The beauteous goatgirl works her way to the top, becoming involved on the way with a Chaldean freedom fighter (Ricardo Montalban) who has early on taken refuge in her lowly hut.

BABYLON—6TH CENTURY B.C.

A new Babylonian/Chaldean Empire did indeed arise, and overthrew Assyria. It descended on Israel, sacked Jerusalem, and carried off a huge number of its citizens into Babylonian captivity. The Babylonian King Belshazzar whose walls were disfigured by cautionary graffiti has been equated with the historical crown prince of Babylon named Bel-shar-utsur. He was the eldest son of Nabonidus, a ruler more interested in excavating ancient Sumerian ruins than in strengthening Babylon; he, his princely son, and Babylon fell to the latest empire builder, Cyrus the Persian, who was to establish the most famous and longlasting Mideastern empire of all.

One of the four intercut story lines in D. W. Griffith's *Intolerance* (1916) centered on the fall of Babylon to Cyrus. His theme of intolerance was here exemplified by kindly, tolerant Prince Belshazzar who is sold out to the Persians by the bigoted High Priest of Bel. Set against this intrigue is a four-cornered love affair: the poet/musician "Rhapsode" (Elmer Clifton) loves the rustically hoydenish mountain girl (Constance Talmadge) who worships at a distance her adored Prince Belshazzar (Alfred Paget) who is happily paired with Attarea, the "Princess Beloved" (Seena Owen). When Cyrus attacks, the mountain girl assumes armor and dies in the defense of her prince.

The immense Babylonian set and breathtaking battle scenes in front of the great walls are memorable in this milestone movie. But there are wonderful details, also, such as the doves pulling tiny wagons of sweets on the princess's table at the great feast.

The Queen of Babylon: The lady in the tutti-frutti hat is not Carmen Miranda, but Rhonda Fleming pretending to be the legendary Semiramis, Queen of Babylon.

28

Intolerance: The gigantic Babylon set engulfed in smoke as the Persians fire the city.

The 300 Spartans: Here are the three hundred, the only Greeks to face the huge army of the Persian King Xerxes.

Opposite and below:

Esther and the King: Richard Egan's appearance is not quite what the historically minded would picture as that of a Persian king-of-kings. Here, as Ahasuerus, he decides that his Queen Vashti (Daniella Rocca) isn't as queenly as she might be. So he replaces her with Esther (Joan Collins), a nice girl from the Jewish community.

GREECE/PERSIA—5TH CENTURY B.C.

In the fifth century B.C., the inhabitants of the mountainous Greek peninsula on the north shore of the Mediterranean had begun to get their act together after the half-millennium of Dark Ages that followed the Heroic Age of the Trojan War. The Persian Empire reached its peak under Darius, but it is his son Xerxes I who is best remembered. It was his mighty army that invaded Greece and was initially resisted only by a minute Spartan force of three hundred at Thermopylae, which was destroyed with but two survivors, an act of heroism renowned through the ages.

Xerxes also appears in the Bible as Ahasuerus in the Book of Esther, which has been gently described as a piece of historical fiction. Nonetheless, it is accurately set in a Persian Empire in which there are still Jewish communities, even after the Jews had been allowed to return to their homeland from the Babylonian exile. When Vashti, the chief wife of Ahasuerus, displeases him, he puts her aside and chooses a new wife from among the beauties of the kingdom. His choice falls on Esther, a Jewish girl. The archvillain of the piece is Haman, a minister to the king, and the story revolves around the struggle between Haman and Esther to influence the king against and for the Jews.

The 300 Spartans (1962) is a sensible, unpretentious movie that does a pretty good job of retelling the story of Leonidas and his tiny army facing the mighty Persian Empire. There's an attempt to convey the complex politics of the Greek city-states, and the Spartan council is cast as the villains, advocating surrender. Nevertheless, Leonidas and his men march off to Thermopylae. The expeditionary force of Xerxes is as lavish as one can desire, including Artemisia of Halicarnassus, a Persian vassal, portrayed as an exotic Oriental lady with Greek sympathies. The battle at Thermopylae is kept as simple as war was then (walk up to an enemy and stab him), with one telling shot of the thin red wedge of Spartans cutting through the black-garbed Persian horde, and there is a suitable sense of place since the film was made on location in Greece.

The strong-jawed Richard Egan is suitably laconic as Leonidas, and Ralph Richardson is the wily Themistocles of Athens.

Richard Egan turns up again in the fifth century B.C. as, of all people, Xerxes/Ahasuerus in *Esther and the King* (1960). Fair-haired and clean-sha-

Alexander the Great: The Persian troops that confronted Alexander's small army. The battle scenes were the best aspect of this ambitious but stiff biography of the first world conqueror.

ven, he's a peculiar picture of a Persian monarch, but then the movie is a peculiar picture of the Persian Empire. Most peculiar of all to our "Dynasty"-trained eyes is Joan Collins as Esther. Just as she is about to be married to her soldier-fiancé, back from the Egyptian wars with Ahasuerus, she is carried off to be part of the beauty contest for Persia's new queen. For somewhat obscure reasons, she takes the fancy of the chief eunuch, who aids her in winning the crown. She learns to love Ahasuerus, a monarch beleaguered by all the intrigues of an Oriental court, and bothered by the upstart Greeks—"Alexander. I'll cut him off in his youth," he mutters presciently, since the boy conqueror is yet to be born.

Alexander the Great: The young Alexander (Richard Burton) has a serious discussion with his father, Philip (Fredric March), despite some attempted distractions.

GREECE—4TH CENTURY B.C.

The astonishing phenomenon known as Alexander the Great inherited the throne of the small, bellicose kingdom of Macedon at twenty years of age. Macedon was on the fringe of Greek civilization, culturally and geographically, and had never played a major role on the Hellenic stage. Alexander was the nexus between the extraordinary new cultural and moral ideas that Greece had produced over the last century, and the semibarbarian militarism of most of the rest of the world. The combination, again combined with astonishing intelligence and beauty, resulted in a young leader who united the city-states of Greece under his rule, then took Egypt, and then proceeded to defeat the greatest empire of the day, the Persian. Using its resources, he went on to India. He died back in Persia, having lived just less than one-third of a century.

His personal life was almost equally dramatic. In his teens, he outshone his militarily brilliant father with predictable resulting conflict. His mother was obsessed with gods whose characters were much less civilized than their Greek counterparts. The enduring love of his life was Haephaestion, a schoolmate under Aristotle. Alexander married twice for policy, once to the daughter of Darius after the Persian conquest to further hopes of uniting the two peoples, once to Roxanne, a princess of Sogdiana, whose father's small kingdom stood in the way on the route to India.

Alexander the Great (1956) takes this amazing story and reduces it mostly to posturing and verbiage, despite the best of intentions. Historically, it is surprisingly accurate in event and production, and certain scenes, such as the decisive battle against the Persians, are beautifully handled.

But the script, in attempting to get in as much of Alexander's crowded career as possible, is choppy. And when it comes down to revealing Alexander on the human level, the results are disastrous. Most successful are the early sections, having to do with Alexander's relations with his volatile parents. This could be due to the strong performances of Fredric March as the rowdy Philip and Danielle Darrieux as the devious, Clytemnestra-like Olympias. Due to the

Hannibal: Hannibal's army copes with an engineering problem involving elephants and Alpine streams.

moral climate of the time that the film was made, there could be no hint of the relationship with Haephaestion, who doesn't even appear among the characters. Instead there is an inflated romance with one Barsine, dubiously reported by Plutarch as having borne a son to Alexander. That this character is played by Claire Bloom at her loveliest makes it only slightly more feasible.

The major problem throughout, however, is Richard Burton, less in performance than in appearance. Even his splendid voice and polished acting could not convince us that here was a gilded youth in his twenties (Burton was thirty-one at the time), and he was further undone by the worst wig ever to undermine a character.

ROME/CARTHAGE—3RD CENTURY B.C.

While the heirs of Alexander squabbled over the divisions of the Empire, two new powers rose to the west. On the south shore of the Mediterranean there was Carthage, a Phoenician colony grown rich on trade. On the north, there was an upstart city on the oddly shaped peninsula called Italy. This city, Rome, grew rich on conquest. The two were bound to collide. They did, in a series of wars called the Punic. Carthage's most extraordinary general was Hannibal, who achieved the feat of attacking Rome from the north by going through Spain and crossing the Alps into Italy, reportedly bringing with him a corps of trained African elephants. Despite this theatrical coup de main, he was eventually beaten by the Romans. Had it not been so, we might well have been speaking a variation of Carthaginian today.

36

Poor Hannibal hasn't fared very well in the movies. There is *Hannibal* (1960), a European-made historical with Victor Mature toward the end of his career. The Carthaginians were given the usual all-purpose Mideastern costuming and sets, and one remains with the memory of Mature slogging through the snows with an elephant or two, repetitively urging the extras to "Keep marching!"

But perhaps an apex of unlikeliness was reached in *Jupiter's Darling* (1955), a musical based on Robert Sherwood's play *The Road to Rome*. It had been one of those amusingly anachronistic theater pieces of the twenties; the film carried anachronism to the point of hilarity. Howard Keel played a singing Hannibal who falls in love with Roman virgin Esther Williams. For collectors of surrealist movie moments, however, there were several in this one: Williams in a submarine fantasy with six pieces of living Greek statuary; Marge and Gower Champion in a song and dance number with a herd of elephants; and an underwater chase sequence of some imagination through grottoes and sunken hulls.

Hannibal: Victor Mature (Hannibal), Rita Gam, and an elephant (left) face the might of Rome together.

Jupiter's Darling: Hannibal (Howard Keel) carries off a Roman bride (Esther Williams) in this thoroughly unlikely look at the Punic Wars.

ROME—1st CENTURY B.C.

Rome inexorably conquered Spain, southern France, Greece, and the eastern shore of the Mediterranean, including Judea. Perhaps the greatest challenge to its military might came not from outside but from inside the growing Empire, when, in 73 B.C., a Thracian gladiator named Spartacus escaped from the gladiatorial school of one Lentulus Batiates at Capua. Raising an army of escaped slaves that eventually numbered 120,000, Spartacus marched first north, seeking to escape over the Alps, then, finding his way blocked by the legions, to the south, in hopes of finding some sort of transport to Sicily or Africa.

Roman citizens were panic stricken; the slave population was enormous, swollen by the prisoners of the wars of conquest, and, inspired by Spartacus, was on the verge of revolt. He had already defeated two armies. Finally, the fabulously

wealthy aristocrat Crassus took command and defeated the slave army. The body of Spartacus was never identified, but six thousand of his men were crucified along the Appian Way from Capua to Rome.

The first century B.C. was a very good century in which to set movies; three such have become classics. *Spartacus* (1960) was one of the last two of the great spectacles, and certainly the most literate. It was based on Howard Fast's novel, which politicized the slave revolt (so far as anyone knows, all Spartacus and his band really wanted was to go home). The film's script kept a remarkable pace. The first half was almost a textbook on the care and training of a gladiator, climaxed by the revolt at the gladiatorial "farm"; the second was the rise of Spartacus's "army" and its pursuit and eventual defeat by Crassus, assisted by the young Julius Caesar. Despite that particular historically dubious detail, the complicated politics of first-century B.C. Rome were made reasonably clear.

This solid narrative was supported by a lavish production and a cast of remarkable actors. Kirk Douglas was a gladiatorial hero par excellence as Spartacus. Jean Simmons, as his slave-girl lover, Varinia, brought a wonderfully touching quality as well as extraordinary looks to her performance ("Has any woman ever looked so beautiful on screen?" asked one critic). Laurence Olivier was a formidable Crassus. Scene stealers Charles Laughton (as Gracchus) and Peter Ustinov (as Batiatus, owner of the gladiators) in one film were almost too much of a good thing, and that future ambassador to Mexico, John Gavin, was photographed to look startlingly like the known busts of the younger Julius Caesar.

EGYPT/ROME—1st CENTURY B.C.

Egypt remained independent under the dynasty established by Alexander's general Ptolemy. When a war broke out between Ptolemy XII and his queen and sister, Cleopatra, it seemed a good opportunity for Rome to step in. Julius Caesar, who had achieved power and popularity with the Roman people through skillful politics and soldiering (having conquered Gaul), made alliance with the young queen, a woman determined to keep Egypt and perhaps take Rome as the consort of the ruler of Rome. Caesar seemed destined to be that ruler. Cleopatra was a formidable lady, intellectually and (apparently) physically. With Caesar's help, she defeated her brother-husband; also with Caesar's help, she bore a child.

Caesar returned to Rome, with intent to make himself sole ruler of the Empire, an aim resented by those who still had hopes of maintaining the centuries-old republican form of government. Adding fuel to the fire was the presence in Rome of Cleopatra and her son, Caesarion. A group of conservatives, including Brutus, supposedly Caesar's bastard son, assassinated Caesar. Caesar's friend, the roistering warrior Marc Antony, hoped to inherit Caesar's power, but Caesar had made a grandnephew, Octavian (later Augustus) his heir. The two combined to defeat Caesar's assassins at the battle of Philippi, and in effect split the Empire between them.

Conflict between the two was inevitable, though, and Antony turned to Egypt for aid. As ruler of the eastern Empire, he ordered Cleopatra to meet him at Tarsus. She received him into her intrigues and her bed, and bore him twins, Alexander Helios and Cleopatra Selene. He returned to Rome to attempt detente, helping this cause by marrying Octavian's sister. The lure of Cleopatra (and her treasury) persisted, he returned to Egypt, and eventually the East (Antony and Cleopatra) faced the West (Octavian) and fought it out in the sea battle of

Spartacus: Products of the Batiatus school of gladiatorial combat (Kirk Douglas, left, and Woody Strode) prepare to show their skill.

Opposite:
Spartacus: The undisciplined army of escaped slaves prepares to meet the *very* disciplined might of Rome.

Cleopatra (1917): The decor in the apartments
of Cleopatra (Theda Bara) was on the busy side
in this silent film version of her life and loves.

Actium, off Greece. Octavian won, and invaded Egypt. After a final hopeless battle, Antony fell on his sword; after a futile plea for clemency to (and perhaps an attempted seduction of) Octavian, Cleopatra arrayed herself in her finest robes and held a poisonous snake to her well-trafficked breast. Octavian killed Caesarion, but brought the twin children of Antony to Rome to be raised by Octavia.

Cleopatra has proved irresistible to the screen since its beginnings—she first appeared in a Georges Méliès short film in 1899. The Serpent of the Nile was a natural for Theda Bara (after all, wasn't her name an anagram for Arab Death?), and she essayed the role in 1917. But the two major *Cleopatras* were from DeMille (1934) and from Joseph L. Mankiewicz (1963), the latter being at that point the most expensive movie ever made. The respective stars were Claudette Colbert (surprising for those familiar only with her comedic image) and Elizabeth Taylor—both brought off the part unforgettably. (*Pace*, Vivien Leigh fans—her praises sung below.)

Right and opposite, above:
Cleopatra (1934): The decor on Cleopatra's barge was also pretty busy in the stylish and witty thirties' view of the Serpent of the Nile. Cleopatra (Claudette Colbert) is putting on the ritz to seduce Marc Antony (Henry Wilcoxon). She didn't, however, expect to fall in love with him.

The form of both is similar, beginning more or less with Caesar's arrival in Egypt and devoting the first half to Caesar and the second to Antony. The DeMille is arguably the best of his movies, lavish, exuberantly (and sometimes unhistorically) imaginative, and showing much of the wit that distinguished his early sound films and was so notably absent in the later ones. The two big "numbers" are Cleopatra's entrance into Rome, fairly restrained by DeMille standards (Egyptian flower girls scattering rose petals at disapproving Roman matrons), and her seduction of Antony on her barge at Tarsus, perhaps the most perfectly paced and artfully composed single scene in all cinema.

It opens with tension—Antony (Henry Wilcoxon) strides into the barge, furious at being kept waiting in the main square of Tarsus, where he's ordered Cleopatra to meet him. It makes a smooth transition to high comedy as Cleopatra shows him all the wonders she had, in her simplicity, prepared to dazzle him: dancing girls, women brought up in nets from the river with handfuls of jewels, virgins riding sacred bulls. (Her barge banqueting hall is just slightly smaller than the Colosseum.) Then a quick dip into low comedy as they both get slightly tiddly (Antony: "I heard someone hiccup." Cleopatra: "Queens

Opposite, below:
Cleopatra (1934). Cleopatra enters Rome with what looked to be a maximum of pomp until the 1963 version came along.

Cleopatra (1963): Cleopatra's welcoming committee in Rome. That's Caesar (Rex Harrison) under the SPQR banner.

Cleopatra (1963): The sixties barge not only floated, it spewed pink smoke.

Opposite:
Cleopatra (1963): In 1963, Cleopatra (Elizabeth Taylor) and her son by Caesar (John Karlsen) entered Rome between the paws of a sphinx only slightly smaller than the one at Giza.

don't hiccup. They only speak of stars."). As Antony finally embraces her, she looks across his shoulder, her face suddenly an icy mask, and nods to her chamberlain. The camera pulls back from their feather-backed dais across the space of the hall. Gauzy drapes fall in front of the dais. Rose petals rain down. Dancing girls writhe. Our point of view, still centered on the dais, pulls further back into a narrow corridor, with sculpted oar-heads projecting from the walls. A drum begins a beat. The oars begin to move. There is a distance shot of the swan-headed barge heading out to sea.

Wilcoxon, the great stone face who appeared in most of DeMille's talkies and starred in several, is surprisingly adept, playing a bluff warrior Antony and serving as a fine foil for Colbert's wit and subtlety. Warren William is an impressively ironic Caesar, and Joseph Schildkraut a memorably devious Herod. But it is Colbert who carries the film. She wears the outrageous deco-Egyptian costumes as if they were Chanel suits. She moves seamlessly from high comedy to dramatic anguish. She is that rarity for an historical epic, a star whose performance succeeds in matching, even outshining, a monumental production.

The later *Cleopatra*, of course, was an even more monumental production. The endless publicity generated by the love life of its stars and its staggering cost was eventually counterproductive; there was an inevitable backlash that has taken a generation to overcome. On current reexamination, it's a literate and beautiful movie, with more than a little witty dialogue and consistently

eye-filling sets and costumes. The first half takes its cue from Shaw, with Rex Harrison as Caesar emphasizing the Shavian connection; he and Taylor's Cleopatra are worthy opponents in their verbal battles. The second, while hardly Shakespearian, is darker and more intense; here Richard Burton is an intelligent, self-doubting Anthony, constantly fighting the shadow of dead Caesar.

The big numbers are again the entrance into Rome and the barge scene, and also the sea battle of Actium against Octavian, which serves as a climax. This time, the barge scene takes second place to the entrance into Rome, if only because the barge is a little more realistically sized—though its progress along the Mediterranean coast, belching pink smoke and paralyzing the local shepherds with awe, would be a high point of any other film. Cleopatra enters the Roman Forum enthroned between the paws of a mobile sphinx about the size of the one at Giza, and alights from its platform on an ingeniously gimbaled litter which doesn't tilt as the slaves bearing it descend the staircase.

The battle of Actium is a truly spectacular effort, the greatest of any such created for the movies. The eye believes these rows of war galleys having at each other, being rammed or going up in flame. For once, there is the rare feeling that if this wasn't the way it was, it should have been.

Costuming manages to be both authentic and beautiful—Taylor seems to have more costumes on her own than the entire rest of the cast, and they range in basic colorization through the entire spectrum. She is not, however, just a rack to hang robes on. Not quite reaching the imperiousness of Colbert, she still conveys a woman seductive, intelligent, and proudly intent on preserving her heritage. She is touching when she realizes that her concern for Antony is real, and she shows a sharp wit (helped by the script: Antony: "I have a fondness for almost all Greek things." Cleopatra: "As an almost all Greek thing myself . . .").

The 1963 Cleopatra is generally credited with being a prime contributor to the demise of the expensive historical spectacular. In retrospect, it's a bum rap—it was an expert exercise in the genre.

There are two major films that are concerned with only part of this story. Shakespeare, in his retelling of the plot to assassinate Caesar, left Cleopatra out of the action entirely. The filming of *Julius Caesar* (1953) made an attempt at historical realism and was given epic treatment. Its mix of accents and styles is bemusing, but there are enough fine performances and moments to make this one of the memorable Shakespeare films. James Mason's Brutus is no less than great; Louis Calhern is a noble Caesar. Deborah Kerr as Portia upholds the British skill at classicism no matter how brief the role, though oddly enough, John Gielgud's Cassius is stiff and so obvious that one wonders how Brutus and Caesar would ever have trusted him. The major point of controversy was Marlon Brando's Antony; could this American "method" actor hold his own? He did, indeed; Antony here is the outsider; the "Cry, havoc" soliloquy over Caesar's body is frighteningly fierce, and the funeral oration a silken incitement to violence, which erupts from hundreds of extras at its end, an effect never possible on stage. Shakespeare would have loved it.

Caesar and Cleopatra (1946) was the most expensive British film ever made; it was spectacular (the re-creation of the Pharos lighthouse, one of the Seven Wonders, was itself a wonder) and it rather neatly combined the screen epic with George Bernard Shaw's witty little play, which has less to do with history than with Shaw's polemics. He supplied the film script and managed to maintain the humor, aided by some fine actors. Claude Rains was a sardonically avuncular Caesar and the youthfully handsome Stewart Granger an Appollodorus (Cleopatra's platonically faithful rug merchant, who carries the carpet in which she is wrapped for delivery to Caesar) so magnetic as to make one

Julius Caesar: Debate raged about the performance of method actor Marlon Brando as Marc Antony; it has stood the test of time.

Opposite, above:
Caesar and Cleopatra: Vivien Leigh turns a silly girl into a queen before our eyes. (The harpist is Jean Simmons.)

Opposite, below left:
Caesar and Cleopatra: Having been instructed in queenship by Caesar (Claude Rains), Cleopatra is confronted by the legions of Rome.

Opposite, below right:
Caesar and Cleopatra: The Romans are coming! The Romans are coming! And the citizens of Alexandria panic.

wonder about Cleopatra's taste in men. The sublimely homely Flora Robson came close to stealing the film as the sinister slave woman, Ftatateeta (the handling of whose name by Caesar was one of the script's running gags). And Vivien Leigh as Cleopatra accomplished the same miracle here as she did in *Gone With the Wind*. She grew from a thoughtless, impulsive girl to a worldly-wise woman before our eyes.

JUDEA—1ST CENTURY A.D.

There are no contemporary references to Jesus apart from the New Testament, but there we are given an unparalleled view of the life of an individual in that period when Rome ruled the world, or what Rome thought was the world. And there are certainly enough historical "hooks" in the New Testament to anchor it firmly into other chronologies. The Roman Republic was dead, killed by imperial expansion beyond which it could not function. The Caesars ruled, and the story indeed starts in the time of "a decree from Caesar Augustus," who was that Octavian who defeated Cleopatra.

Rome, despite its future reputation, was hardly an evil empire by the standards of its day. Slavery was an expected concomitant of conquest and empire, and a ruling conqueror was expected to exact tribute from defeated nations. And Rome did follow the relatively enlightened precedent of Alexander in allowing a conquered country its own religion and rule by collaborators of its own culture.

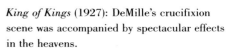

King of Kings (1927): DeMille's crucifixion scene was accompanied by spectacular effects in the heavens.

Marc Antony had installed as the civil rulers of the Roman province of Judea the Herod family, Idumeans from the south who were Jewish in religion but still considered outsiders by the nationalistic Judeans, who took particular exception to the marriage customs of the Herods. Herodias, the granddaughter of Herod the Great, married and divorced one of his sons, her uncle, and then married another, Herod Antipas, tetrarch (courtesy of Rome) of Galilee. A holy man called John the Baptist, inheritor of the tradition of Judean prophets, denounced the marriage as incestuous, not because Herodias was the niece of Herod Antipas, but because she had been his half-brother's wife. Herod Antipas was hesitant to execute John for fear of further arousing public opinion, but Herodias's daughter by her first marriage (unnamed in the Bible, but called Salome by the historian Josephus) so pleased him by her dancing that she was promised anything she asked. She asked, of course, for the head of John the Baptist.

The movies set in the time of Christ are of several varieties. Some are biographies of Jesus, others center on persons connected with him (Peter, Barabbas) or on fictional characters from his parables (the prodigal son) or invented to interact with his story (Ben Hur).

A life of Jesus was made as early as 1912, but the first major depiction of Jesus on screen was in D. W. Griffith's *Intolerance*. There three episodes from Christ's life were shown as one of the four intercut stories depicting intolerance through the ages.

King of Kings (1961): A buffet banquet for the Jerusalem upper class, including Pilate (Hurd Hatfield), Herod (Gregoire Aslan), and Salome (Brigid Bazlen), doesn't seem to be going well.

King of Kings (1961): The Romans prepare to invade the Tabernacle in Jerusalem.

Opposite, above:
King of Kings (1961): The problem of seating an uneven number at table was neatly solved in this version of the Last Supper.

Opposite, below:
The Greatest Story Ever Told: The costumes in this biography of Jesus, wtih a few exceptions, were in deliberately muted earth tones, as in this crowd scene of the entrance of Jesus (Max Von Sydow) into Jerusalem.

It was Cecil B. DeMille who first gave the life of Jesus the superspectacular treatment in *The King of Kings* (1927) which *The New York Times*'s Mordaunt Hall called "the most impressive of all motion pictures" at the time. It's somehow typical that DeMille would begin the picture with a feast at Mary Magdalene's house. Her current favorite, Judas Iscariot, has apparently discovered a subsequent engagement, however. Indignant, the Magdalene goes in search of him, and finds him with an unexpected rival, a man of God. It is, of course, Jesus, and from there we are shown various episodes of Jesus' life from the raising of Lazarus through the Crucifixion. Jesus was portrayed by distinguished stage and screen actor H. B. Warner, whose career stretched through the sound era, where he played many a suave financier and scientist, to the 1956 *The Ten Commandments*.

The next big treatment of the life of Jesus was also titled *King of Kings* (1961), but was not by DeMille. Here the story was given a speedy, comic book, great-moments-from-the-life-of approach; Orson Welles supplies a somewhat lugubrious narration. It was visually of the calendar pictorial school, typified by the use of the handsome young actor Jeffrey Hunter as an auburn-haired, blue-eyed Jesus; the emphasis was definitely on the gentle human side.

Much of the script was filled in with fictional material (historically distorted in places—Pilate's wife is here the Emperor Tiberius's daughter). Action is supplied with an invented subplot in which Barabbas is a Jewish rebel against Rome and Judas a cohort. Barabbas hopes to use Jesus' following in an uprising, and Judas's motive for the betrayal is the attempt to force Jesus' hand in that direction. Sex is of course supplied by the old reliable Herod/Salome situation—Salome (Brigid Bazlen) is depicted as a precociously sexy mid-adolescent, more a rival to Herodias (Rita Gam in exotically baroque robes) than a coconspirator. Siobhan McKenna brought a touch of class to the whole business as a serenely radiant, peasant-featured Mary.

Hard on the heels of *King of Kings* came *The Greatest Story Ever Told* (1965) which was an extraordinarily beautiful movie. Instead of grandiose sets, George Stevens chose to use the spectacular scenery of the American West to

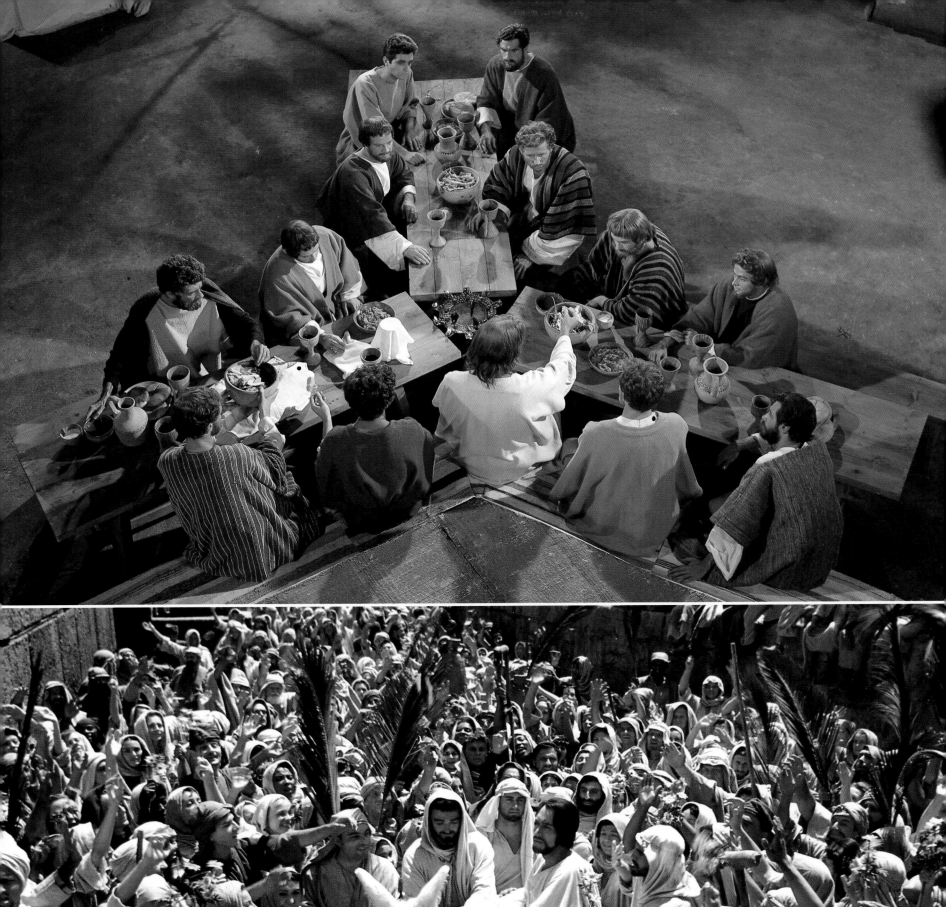

Opposite:
The Greatest Story Ever Told: The magnificent
scenery of the American West took the place of
lavish sets, and did so very effectively.

The Gospel According to St. Matthew: The
crucifixion as shown in this reverently simple
film about Jesus' life taken from the first
Gospel.

stand in for the landscapes of Judea as a backdrop for the story of Jesus. It was
an inspired idea, enhanced by a deliberate use of muted colors for costumes
and buldings. Actors and extras are dressed in white, cream, tan, and grays,
with black for the heavies—Herod's military and much of the Sanhedrin.
Against this, the occasional vivid color—the wine of Herod's robe, the red of
Pilate's uniform, the green of Herodias's dress—makes its own statement.

It's unfortunate that the script could not match the visual style. Immensely
respectful, it has an almost perverse tendency to dwell on Jesus' more cryptic
utterances, and while it avoids the vulgarity of *King of Kings*, the results are
slow and often oblique, conveying little of the drama, passion, and joy of the
story.

There were interesting touches, however. Donald Pleasance appeared as a
character called "the Dark Hermit," the one who shows Jesus the kingdoms of
the Earth from the mountaintop; he reappears periodically at critical moments—the call for the stoning of the woman taken in adultery (here the
Magdalene), Peter's denial of Jesus, and leading the shouts of "Crucify him" at
the trial—representing the darker elements aligned against Jesus. And the
feast during which John the Baptist is beheaded is a riveting scene. The wiles
of Herodias and her daughter are not specified, though the two are present.
Herod sits alone in his darkened throne room with the music of the feast and
the shadows of the dancers in the background. Salome enters and dances in a
white shift in and out of the shafts of light thrown by the torches, looking like a
demented butterfly as the axe falls on John.

Any number of stars and demi-stars appeared in cameo roles, to greater or
lesser effect. Dorothy McGuire also excelled in the serene radiance depart-
ment as Mary; Claude Rains was a wily monster as the elder Herod; Ed Wynn,
of all people, was a blind man given sight. Michael Anderson, Jr., played an
appealingly adolescent James the Younger, bringing some much needed light-
ness to the proceedings, and John Wayne had one growled line as the Roman
centurion in charge of the crucifixion. Max Von Sydow was a sternly impressive, not-very-human Jesus, more Father than Son.

There have been less ambitious, and perhaps more effective, films on the
life of Christ. Pier Paolo Pasolini's *The Gospel According to St. Matthew* (1966)
was a low-keyed, realistic version that, as the title suggests, drew entirely on
the first gospel and by its very modesty seemed more suited to its subject. The
controversial *The Last Temptation of Christ* (1988) riled many Christians and

Overleaf:
The Last Temptation of Christ: Willem Dafoe
was a controversially human Jesus in this story
of Christ.

Salome (1953): Rita Hayworth, well swathed in all seven veils, begins her dance. The choreography was by the noted modern dancer Valerie Bettis.

delighted others by emphasizing the humanity of Jesus to the extent of show-ing, as fantasies on the cross, his desire to lay down the burden of divinity and live the life of an ordinary mortal, including marriage.

Major among the persons peripheral to Jesus who have had movies built around them is, of course, Salome, mainly because she is one of the few whose story can have some sex extrapolated into it. Theda Bara inevitably played the role (in 1918), but the most celebrated of the Salome films is the 1923 silent version of Oscar Wilde's play, conceived and with art direction by Valentino's wife, Natacha Rambova. She based the entire look of the film on Aubrey Beardsley's drawings, and the result is a delirious overdose of art nouveau, a phantasmagoria of sinuous sets and costumes that is one of the most bizarre movies ever made. The celebrated Nazimova was a beautiful and graceful Salome so far as one can see under the white wigs and ball-fringe headdresses.

Bizarre in another way was Rita Hayworth's *Salome* (1953). On the then-operative theory that a star could not play a thoroughly bad character, the script portrayed Salome as a sort of Galilean Gilda, a good-bad girl who did it all for love of her mother and thought she was dancing not to end John's life, but to save it. (This took some pretty fancy stepping on the part of the script-writers as well.) The celebrated modern dancer Valerie Bettis supplied the surprisingly effective choreography for Hayworth's veil removal. Herodias was played by Judith Anderson at her most sinister, and Charles Laughton almost mugged the picture into life as Herod. Stewart Granger was the Roman officer with whom Salome ended up holding hands at the Sermon on the Mount. (In keeping with family tradition, the historical Salome reportedly married her great-uncle Philip.)

Opposite, above:
Salomé (1923): Salome (Nazimova) at the pit wherein John the Baptist is incarcerated.

Opposite, below:
Salomé (1923): *The* dance executed by Nazimova in this experiment in totally stylized cinema based on the Aubrey Beardsley drawings for the Oscar Wilde play.

The apostle Peter, played by the rugged Royal Dano in the second *King of Kings* and the sensitive Gary Raymond in *The Greatest Story*, had his own movie in the seemingly endless *The Big Fisherman* (1959). Baritone musical star Howard Keel took time off from pursuing Kathryn Grayson and Esther Williams (once as Hannibal—see above) to portray Peter, and brought some sensitivity and dignity to the role. Since Peter by tradition went on to Rome, he would reappear in films dealing with Christianity's emergence in that city, played by actors as divergent as Michael Rennie (*The Robe* and *Demetrius and the Gladiators*), Lorne Green (*The Silver Chalice*), and Finlay Currie (*Quo Vadis*).

The Big Fisherman: Howard Keel as Peter, "the big fisherman," actually managed to bring some dignity to a sodden screenplay.

As a character, Barabbas, the criminal who was freed instead of Jesus by Pilate in honor of Passover, would seem slightly less charismatic than Peter or Salome. But so little is said of him that his story is open to any sort of extrapolation, and Par Lagerkvist chose him as the central figure of a novel fraught with guilt and redemption. The film *Barabbas* (1962), based on the novel, is a dour epic indeed. Anthony Quinn does his best as the inarticulate hero who goes from the silver mines to the gladiatorial arena, becoming a Christian on the way. The background has a certain amount of originality since much of the action takes place in what might be called the Jerusalem underworld.

Hollywood transformed the simple parable of the prodigal son into epic silliness in *The Prodigal* (1955). The original story was totally unspecific as to time and place. The movie is set in Joppa and Damascus in 70 B.C. Its plot is singlemindedly concerned with the unrelieved lust of Edmund Purdom, as a Jewish youth, for Lana Turner as Samarra, the high priestess of Astarte in Damascus. He first sees her in a sort of missionary tent show that the heathens put on in Joppa, presumably to tempt the good citizens. Purdom immediately takes his inheritance and decamps to Damascus, where he is subjected to such indignities as being made a slave and fighting a maddened buzzard. He eventually leads a revolt against the theocracy, and Samarra falls into the flaming pool of sacrifice. All in all, it had the quality of a preliminary sketch for a Conan movie.

Later writers conceived the idea of inventing characters who would interact with the events of the New Testament. One of the first of these was Lew Wal-

Opposite, above:
Barabbas: "There but for . . ." Anthony Quinn is Barabbas in this stark film about the thief who was released in place of Jesus.

Opposite, below:
The Prodigal: Lana Turner, as the high priestess of Astarte, travels in style.

Ben Hur (1959): The Roman fleet, propelled by Ben and other galley slaves.

lace, Union general of the Civil War, who wrote of a Judean prince whose melodramatic life was touched by Jesus several times. The novel was called *Ben-Hur*. It made its way to the stage, where the climactic chariot race was done for the audience with horses madly galloping on a treadmill. It was first filmed in 1907, but the BIG version came along in 1926. A problem production, it was literally years in the making, but the end result was indeed colossal.

Prince Judah Ben-Hur has learned to live with the Romans, but is wounded when his boyhood friend, the Roman officer, Messala, shows prejudice on his return to Jerusalem. Hur accidentally dislodges a roof tile while watching the entrance of the new Roman governor, and is responsible for his death. He is sentenced to the galleys and on the way there as part of a chain gang of slaves, he is given water and hope by a young carpenter in Nazareth.

During a fierce battle at sea against pirates, his galley is breached but he manages to save the life of the commander of the Roman forces, who in gratitude adopts him. Hur makes every effort to find his mother and sister, but eventually assumes that they are dead. He returns to Judea to investigate his inheritance, and falls in love with Esther, the daughter of the steward of the Hur estates.

He is befriended by a Bedouin sheik, and drives his horses against Messala in the circus at Antioch; the Roman is killed in the fierce competition. On the word of the mage Balthazar, Hur's winnings are put toward raising an army for Jesus, the young carpenter now preaching in the city. Jesus is condemned to death, and on the way to his crucifixion cures Hur's mother and sister, who have been released from the dungeon where they have been secretly incarcerated, and who are suffering from leprosy. Hur disbands his army.

Every possible excuse for spectacle was drawn from this operatic scenario, from the opening shot of Jerusalem's Joppa Gate to the gigantic circus at Antioch. The sea battle is still astonishing when viewed today, and though the photography for the chariot race is primitive to our eyes, it has a reality and a presence that the later version lacks. Ramon Novarro was at his best, going from effete young prince to sophisticated man of action. Francis X. Bushman

Opposite, above:
Ben-Hur (1926): A chariot bites the dust in front of a colossal figure on the *spina* of the Antioch Colosseum.

Opposite, below:
Ben-Hur (1926): There was full employment for the extras of Hollywood when the chariot race of the first *Ben-Hur* was filmed.

Ben-Hur (1926): A battle between the Roman Navy and pirates was one of the big moments.

Ben Hur (1959): The villain Messala (Stephen Boyd) has the black horses, of course; Ben Hur (Charlton Heston) is piloting the white.

The Robe: Ernest Thesiger (right) was a kinder, gentler Tiberius Caesar than history records. Here, watched by his beautiful ward Diana (Jean Simmons), he tries to persuade the tribune Marcellus (Richard Burton) that his reactions to the Crucifixion are psychological.

made a heavyjawed Messala. May McAvoy was, in the style of the time, an insipid Esther with Pickford curls; Carmel Myers stole the show on the female side as the platinum-wigged Egyptian vamp, Iras.

As no one needs to be told, *Ben Hur* (without the hyphen) was remade in 1959 and had everything its predecessor did except flair. It was a monumentally stolid production matched by the monumentally stolid performance of its star, Charlton Heston. It seemed typical of the script that there was no bad woman in it (it made one aware of just how much a Messalina or a Poppaea can enliven history); the only real feminine interest was supplied by Haya Harareet as the tepid Esther. (The Israeli actress's career did not take off after her introduction to an international audience in *Ben Hur.* Heston's generally good reviews prompted the rather unfair joke "Loved Ben, hated her.")

Stephen Boyd tried mightily as Messala, but his cleft chin didn't quite carry the weight of Bushman's heavy jaw. Hugh Griffith managed some flamboyance as Sheik Ilderim and won an Academy Award for it, as did Heston, the director William Wyler, and the picture itself, which was also the top grossing movie for 1960. It made more than twice as much as the second film of that year, *Psycho,* and also grossed more than would *Spartacus* and *Cleopatra,* both then in early production.

Perhaps the best known of all the movies concerning Jesus is *The Robe* (1953), but not because it's the best. This was the movie that introduced that

television-busting wide-screen process, Cinemascope, to movie-going audiences, and publicity-inspired curiosity about the gimmick accounted for much of its grosses. From a best-selling novel by Lloyd C. Douglas, it's the story of the Roman tribune who headed the execution detail in charge of the Crucifixion.

It is this Marcellus who wins Jesus' garment in the dice game. When he dons it to escape the storm brought on by the Crucifixion, it evokes a violent physical and psychological response: he flings it from his back. His Greek slave, Demetrius, who has become a follower of Jesus, takes it and escapes.

Back in Rome, Marcellus is convinced that he is going mad because of continued psychological problems connected with the events in Jerusalem. The aged Tiberius Caesar is sympathetic; his court magician diagnoses the problem as a spell cast by the robe, which Marcellus must find. Tiberius assigns him to return to Palestine as an imperial agent, to gather knowledge on the new sect as well as to seek out the robe. Marcellus finds Demetrius and the robe in the company of Peter and becomes a convert. The three go to Rome, where the new Caesar, Caligula, is beginning the persecution of Christians.

Demetrius is captured and tortured. Marcellus rescues him, but he appears dead. Peter appears and Demetrius revives. Marcellus is captured helping Demetrius escape, and is condemned to death by Caligula.

Wide the movie may have been, but deep it was not. The hokum of the plot was presented with a poker-faced pietism that allowed not a breath of life to infuse any of the characters, and the production was monumentally dull—the large size of the screen was apparently to make up for the small size of the sets. The biggest thrill for the audience came in the chase, in which Demetrius and Marcellus are pursued in a carriage drawn by four white horses abreast, photographed head-on. This may have been Cinemascopically effective, but seemed an odd way to harness a team.

It is here that we begin to meet the parade of Caesars by which the numerous films set in first-century Rome will be characterized. Ernest Thesiger was less dithery than usual as Tiberius; not, perhaps, the bluff, decadent old warrior of history, but cynically wise. ("This is how it will start . . . some obscure martyr in some forgotten province," he says of Rome's end.) Jay Robinson was so hysterically unstable as Caligula that one could only wonder why the decline and fall took another couple of centuries.

Demetrius and the Gladiators: Caligula (Jay Robinson, center) has words with his successor-to-be, Claudius (Barry Jones) and his wife, Messalina (Susan Hayward).

THE ROMAN EMPIRE—1ST CENTURY A.D.

This was the century of the famous—and infamous—Caesars. The dour Tiberius followed the Divine Augustus, to be followed in turn by the young Caligula, the old Claudius, and the artistic Nero (the succession was not from father to son, but accomplished by an increasingly arbitrary system of adoption and support by various power groups). Contrary to popular belief (fostered by the movies), the Romans and their emperors did not spend most of their time tracking down Christians and then doing vile things to them in torture chambers and the arena. There seems to be no clear evidence of anything in the way of specific persecution until the time of Nero. Even then (and thereafter) it was sporadic and not just confined to Christianity. Rome was sociologically aware enough to be worried about alien beliefs undermining the Roman way of life (the Gods, Roman mothers, and the Roman equivalent of apple pie), a phenomenon hardly confined to that age or that Empire. A modern equivalent might be the attitude of the American middle class of the first half of this century toward Bolshevism.

The Caesars and their families provided a gaudy counterpoint with an increasingly luxurious life-style shared by many of the patricians and inhibited by little in the way of morals or law. Claudius, whose accession to the throne occurred mainly because he was on hand when Caligula's assassination at the

hands of the Praetorian Guard provided the need for a successor, was something of an exception, a scholar and a capable administrator. But his wife Messalina more than made up for his comparative circumspection.

Total power corrupted Caligula and Nero; the latter was so thoroughly preoccupied with his musical and theatrical pursuits that little serious governing was done at all. Nero replaced his chaste wife Octavia with the vicious Sabina Poppaea; when his mother, the scheming Agrippina, objected (probably sensing a powerful rival), he had her killed. Poppaea soon died, reportedly from a kick to the stomach while pregnant. There was eventually a revolt in Gaul, and even the Senate turned against Nero, less because of his excesses than because he insisted on making a public spectacle of himself by giving vocal concerts. He killed himself (with a little help from a friend) while hiding from the Senate's soldiers in the cellar of a rural villa.

Demetrius and the Gladiators (1954) was based on a character created by Lloyd C. Douglas in *The Robe*, the music was by Franz Waxman but with themes by Alfred Newman from *The Robe*, and several of the sets were recycled from the 1953 movie. In other words, it's a sort of second-hand *Robe*. But it's a good deal more fun than the original, due to some well-staged contests in the arena,

I, Claudius: A family banquet with the vicious Caligula (Emlyn Williams, left), the beautiful Messalina (Merle Oberon), and Uncle Claudius (Charles Laughton).

and the presence of a wicked woman, in this case Messalina, portrayed by Susan Hayward.

The film opens during the reign of Caligula; Jay Robinson repeats his role, chewing up what's left of the scenery. The freed Greek slave, Demetrius (Victor Mature), is returned to slavery, this time at the gladiatorial school owned by Claudius in which Claudius's wife, Messalina, takes a great interest. Demetrius won't fight, but eventually disillusioned by the death of a young girl at the hands of his fellow gladiators, he becomes top man in the arena and spends a lot of time at Messalina's seaside villa.

Caligula, in the meantime, is searching for the wonder-working robe of Christ and sends Demetrius to get it. He finds that the girl is alive (Peter has been by). Demetrius's faith is restored, but he takes the robe to Caligula. With it, Caligula tries to raise the dead, but with no instruction manual, fails, and it's back to the arena with Demetrius. Again in the pacifist Christian mode, Demetrius is about to get the thumbs-down from Caligula, but the Praetorian Guard is on his side, and Caligula gets a spear thrust instead. Claudius ascends the throne and Messalina, in the most historically laughable scene of either film, repents her wicked, wicked ways and promises to be a good wife and empress.

During most of its history, the cinema hadn't been very successful at portraying the decadent and corrupt Rome of the Caesars; due to censorship, it could only hint with varying degrees of success. Most screen orgies were rather

I, *Claudius:* Claudius realizes that Caligula has become a god and pays due homage.

proper affairs. *Caligula* (1980) was probably much closer to the real nastiness that underlay much of imperial Roman society; unfortunately it went so far in the other direction, being a virtually unending visual catalogue of sex acts (natural and un-) and bloodletting (often combined with the sex), that it was virtually unwatchable.

It traces the rule of Caligula from his involvement in the murder of his predecessor, Tiberius, in his retreat at Capri (shown here as one unending orgy) to Caligula's own assassination. It says something for the film that the only remotely tender passion shown throughout is Caligula's incestuous love for his sister Drusilla. (And it is indeed shown, with no holds barred, including a touch of necrophilia after her death.) Under other circumstances, Malcolm McDowell would have been an ideal Caligula with a hint of the foul underlying his perpetually boyish quality. It's not quite worth sticking through the endlessly churning pornography to see the excellent actress Helen Mirren as Caligula's wife and some extraordinarily handsome sets. Caligula, in short, is really just the world's most expensive ($15 million) porn movie.

We owe to the BBC whatever knowledge that we have of the most famous unfinished film of all time, Alexander Korda's *I, Claudius* from the two-part "autobiography" of Claudius Caesar by Robert Graves. Graves had painted a horrendous portrait of Rome in the first century A.D. as seen through the eyes of Claudius, and in particular the malevolent maneuvering for power to which the relatives and descendants of Augustus had resorted. The prime villain was

I, *Claudius:* Portrait of an emperor-to-be. Unfinished the film may have been, but anyone who has seen the extant fragments will vouch for the greatness of Laughton's performance.

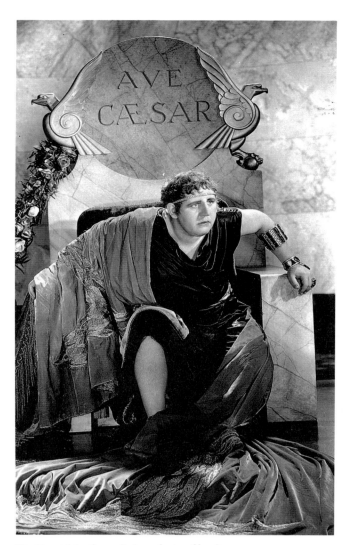

The Sign of the Cross: Before playing Claudius, Charles Laughton essayed a plump and pallid Nero for Cecil B. DeMille.

Opposite, above:

The Sign of the Cross: Poppaea (Claudette Colbert), Nero's consort, takes what may be the most lavish bath in screen history. The milk is ass's.

Opposite, below:

The Sign of the Cross: The Roman games staged for the film were anything but Little League. That's Nero and Poppaea (Laughton and Colbert) up there under the eagle.

Augustus's wife, Livia, who literally stopped at nothing to gain the throne for her son, Tiberius. While this was purely Graves's invention, he had taken historical characters and the facts of the times and manners of their deaths and woven a highly plausible web of intrigue. It was Graves's conceit that Claudius had the good sense to survive the wholesale slaughter of family members by pretending to be a simpleton.

The movie was to be a monumental production, and a month of filming was accomplished before the project was abandoned. The superb cast included Charles Laughton as Claudius, Flora Robson as Livia, Merle Oberon as Messalina, and Emlyn Williams as Caligula. Enough footage survives (collected by the BBC into a documentary called "The Epic That Never Was") to show that the production was indeed a splendid one, and that Laughton was giving a performance the likes of which had probably never been seen on screen before. His pathetic Claudius, limping and stuttering, incorporated the pathos of the future portrayal of the hunchback of Notre Dame with an underlying sly intelligence and humor. Luckily, the scene in which he takes control of the Senate after Caligula's death was shot before the close of production; it is the triumph of an intellectual butterfly emerging from an idiot's cocoon before one's eyes.

Accounts of the problems vary, but there seems to be the general view that Laughton and the director, Josef von Sternberg, had no empathy whatsoever and specifically that von Sternberg was not supplying Laughton with the support the actor always so badly needed (perhaps to excess). In any case, the irreplaceable Oberon's involvement in an auto accident seemed to give everyone the out that was wanted. The production was aborted and reportedly Lloyd's of London paid a fortune in insurance.

Laughton had brought off another Caesarian tour de force earlier in De-Mille's *The Sign of the Cross* (1932) as Nero, everybody's favorite Caesar. Given the director, subtlety was not a major feature of any part of the film, but Laughton's petulant lyre-playing Nero was vastly amusing, as was Claudette Colbert at her most glamorous as an acid-tongued Poppaea. Her current interest is the playboy prefect of Rome, Marcus Superbus (Fredric March with exquisitely curled hair). He in turn has eyes only for Mercia, a lovely girl he has met in a poor district of the city, played by the horrendously ladylike Elissa Landi; of course she is a Christian. Nero blames the Christians for the fire that has destroyed Rome and rounds them up for inventively lethal displays in the arena. Marcus joins Mercia in martyrdom.

Despite a rousing Rome-is-burning section, the two sequences that captured the audience were Colbert's bath and the "games" of the arena. With a strident "hee haw" on the soundtrack, the bath scene starts with asses being milked and the buckets emptied into a conduit; the milk flows from exquisite faucets into Poppaea's swimming-pool-sized tub. Colbert is immersed up to the neck, and the milk is of course opaque. In a conversation with a lady of the court, however, she makes some dangerously revealing waves. The scene concludes with a telling shot of two cats lapping the liquid from the side of the pool. Already known for his bathtub scenes, DeMille set out to top them (and succeeded) with this.

His inventiveness extended to the various bloodthirsty games of the arena. Probably the most memorable was the squad of blonde barbarian women fighting to the death against a troupe of black dwarfs (one woman spits a dwarf on her trident and holds him triumphantly aloft).

The Sign of the Cross was adapted from a play by Wilson Barrett; this playwright had also adapted a turn-of-the-century novel called *Quo Vadis?* for the stage, and the plots of the two are very similar. Both have a Roman officer

Quo Vadis: A citizen's eye view of the ceremonies accompanying the Roman Triumph.

Overleaf:

Quo Vadis: Not quite the largest of monumental sets, but certainly the most effectively used, was the re-creation of a Roman Triumph.

Opposite, above:

The Silver Chalice: Whatever his faults, Nero certainly gave full employment to cooks, sculptors, and acrobats for his social events, to judge from this view.

Opposite, below left:

The Silver Chalice: The seductress Helena (Virginia Mayo) attempts to distract sculptor Basil (Paul Newman). The set, purporting to be Nero's banqueting hall, was certainly stylish if not realistic.

Opposite, below right:

The Silver Chalice: There were two reasons to see *The Silver Chalice.* One was a newcomer to the screen named Paul Newman, seen here dallying with Pier Angeli. The other was the wonderfully stylized sets, such as this "street" in Damascus.

falling for a Christian girl in the time of Nero, with the fire serving as a catalyst for the climax in the arena. *Quo Vadis?* was turned into a spectacular silent film in Italy in 1924, with Emil Jannings as Nero. A quarter of a century later, in 1951, it became one of the biggest of the biggies.

Robert Taylor was the Roman officer, unoriginally named Marcus. An aging idol at this point, his portrayal of a rather stolid, humorless Roman was perhaps too right on the mark. The beautiful red-haired Deborah Kerr was the Christian Lygia, adopted daughter to a patrician Roman family; like other British actresses in similar roles, she actually created a character from almost nothing. Peter Ustinov's Nero was an hysterical paranoid, coming dangerously close to caricature, but never quite crossing the line. Patricia Laffan's petulant Poppaea was notable mostly for her towering hairdos; she lacked Colbert's wit as well as her bathtub. The most solidly interesting character in the movie was Petronius, the arbiter of fashion of Nero's court, as played by Leo Genn. Not quite so airily elegant as the original, he still provided some much needed subtlety and humor while coping with Nero's childish tantrums, and some authentic pathos and courage while calmly feasting with friends before killing himself at Nero's displeasure.

While much of *Quo Vadis* seems stodgy and a little slow-moving, one scene must be noted, that of the triumph of Marcus's legions held in the Roman Forum. The set is dominated by colossal figures of the gods, which dwarf the thousands of extras through which the procession makes its way. Several shots, from a high and oblique angle showing the entire Forum, are unmatched before or since for sheer awe-inspiring spectacle.

The Silver Chalice (1954) was certainly one of the more stiffly ludicrous spectaculars of the Nero *vs.* Christians school, but it had its interesting and unusual aspects. For one, Paul Newman made his screen debut in the lead; his star qualities were immediately apparent despite the material he had to work with. For another, there were no arena scenes and the convertible Roman officer was missing, though there was a pretty Christian girl (Pier Angeli), granddaughter of Joseph of Arimathea. Newman is Basil, a cynical Greek slave-sculptor commissioned to make a chalice to hold the cup from the Last Supper.

Above and opposite:
The Last Days of Pompeii: The Roman town's
last days were rather spectacular, both at sea
and on land.

Pitted against this enterprise is Simon the Magician (Jack Palance), who
wants to surpass Jesus' achievements as a miracle-worker. (Simon is mentioned in the Bible, and is thought to have founded a Phrygian gnostic sect, the
Atsigani, from which the word for gypsy—"Tziganer"—comes.) He has a
luscious assistant, Helena (Virginia Mayo), the equivalent of the lady that
modern stage magicians saw in half. She and the nice Christian girl compete
for Basil and his soul, as he struggles to complete the chalice. They all end up
in Rome, where Simon performs before Nero and claims to be able to fly;
ovecome with megalomania, he tries it with no reliance on the planned devices
and, needless to say, fails fatally.

The other surprise that the movie had to offer was an astonishingly stylized
production that made little effort toward historical veracity and a lot toward
sets and costumes that wouldn't have looked out of place at an avant-garde
dance performance. Particularly notable were the roofscape of Damascus, an
endless moonscape of white domes, and Nero's banqueting hall, a huge area of
king-sized dining couches surrounded by an infinity of golden arches containing classical statuary. This visual madness extended to minute details of
costume, such as Mayo's nearly-vertical eyebrows, and the thin golden halo-
like headband worn by Angeli. The results were eccentric, but a great relief
from the stiff "realism" of such productions as *The Robe.*

The Last Days of Pompeii (1935) had almost nothing to do with Bulwer-
Lytton's famous novel, but the title still told it all. Preston Foster plays yet
another Marcus; this one has worked his way up from blacksmith to master

The Fall of the Roman Empire: The funeral of
Marcus Aurelius at Vindobona (Vienna), here
attended by his daughter Lucilla (Sophia Loren)
and her suitor, Livius (Stephen Boyd).

gladiator in the arena of the provincial town of Pompeii. (The local ruler is
Pontius Pilate, transferred back here from Jerusalem.) Alas, Marcus's son
wants to be a Christian instead of a gladiator (you guessed it—there's a lovely
Christian girl involved), and the climax features games in the arena involving
Christians and gladiators, interrupted by earthquake and eruption. All (arena,
earthquake, eruption) are satisfyingly spectacular.

THE ROMAN EMPIRE—2ND CENTURY A.D.

*After Nero, a certain amount of stability was achieved in the Roman Empire for
a hundred years. But around the end of the second century A.D., cracks began to
appear. The reign of the stoic philosopher-king Marcus Aurelius was beset with
plague and rebellion, and he set the decline and fall in motion by naming as heir
his son, Commodus, who preferred to be a gladiatorial rather than a philosphi-
cal king (and a skillful one, according to all reports—hundreds of kills to his
credit). Commodus brought back all the horrors of Nero and Caligula, and was
strangled in his bath by his favorite wrestling partner.*

The Fall of the Roman Empire (1964) was a bit anticipatory in its title; the
complete decline and fall took centuries, and the movie only covers the beginning of the process, taking as its plot the death of Marcus Aurelius (Alec
Guinness), the romance of his daughter Lucilla (Sophia Loren) with the up-

The Fall of the Roman Empire: One of the great sets depicting Rome, this was manufactured in Spain.

standing Livius (Stephen Boyd), and the ascension to the throne of Commodus (Christopher Plummer) to everyone's dismay.

A fairly intelligent script (helped no end by the full weight of Guinness's intelligence as a believable Marcus Aurelius) still could not avoid over-talkiness, which was now and then relieved by some excellent action sequences (another chariot race for Stephen Boyd, veteran of *Ben Hur*) and two very impressive sets: the Roman fortifications at Vindobona (Vienna), scene of Aurelius's death, and the Roman Forum. The latter was said to have been the largest set ever built, but it was less well used than the Forum of *Quo Vadis*. The costumes were interestingly accurate; the armor of the soldiers already anticipated the look of medieval knights.

Plummer as Commodus did a good deal to liven things up, but the dreary romance between Livius and an historically misrepresented Lucilla (she was apparently as much of a monster as her brother) made one suspect that the Empire fell from boredom rather than decadence.

THE MIDDLE AGES

THE ROMAN EMPIRE—4TH CENTURY A.D.

The Roman Empire took a while to decline and fall, but by the fourth century A.D. it was simply a battleground for warring rival Caesars. Momentarily Constantine I got it all together (having to conquer Rome to do it), but the reunification didn't last past his death. However, in establishing Constantinople as the new capital, he succeeded in starting the Byzantine Empire, with Christianity as its state religion. Ah, Nero, had you but known?

The story of *Constantine and the Cross* (1962) took a conventionally pious view of the Emperor's conversion to Christianity, which in reality was probably more of a political than a theological move. Cornel Wilde was an impassive Constantine squaring off against the remaining pagan Romans. The big scene is the Battle of the Mulvian Bridge, the one before which Constantine saw the flaming cross in the sky captioned "In this sign, conquer." Needless to say, the movie audience was treated to the same sight.

Fabiola (1947) was an Italian attempt just after World War II to regain preeminence in the field of historical spectaculars. It didn't succeed, but the film itself had a slightly harder edge than the American examples, even though it replayed the familiar story of Romans plotting against Christians, this time on the eve of Constantine's capture of the city. The orgies were sophisticated by the standards of the time, and the stunning French actress Michele Morgan was a Christian heroine with some depth.

THE BYZANTINE EMPIRE—5TH CENTURY A.D.

Matters in Europe were not helped in the fifth century by the advance of the Huns from the eastern steppes. Their king, Attila, speeded up this advance into conquest and shook both the Byzantine Empire and what was left of the Roman.

Kings of the Sun: The young Mayan king (George Chakiris, top left) standing on the newly built pyramid is saluted by his people.

Fabiola: Circumspect by today's standards, the orgies in this Italian film were still racier than Hollywood's of the period.

A bizarre incident in Attila's career is the central theme of *Sign of the Pagan* (1954). Honoria, sister of the Western Roman emperor, had been banished because of some hanky-panky with a court chamberlain. Taking refuge in the Eastern capitol, she sent a ring to Attila with a plea for help. Attila (who apparently had a sense of humor) chose to interpret this as an offer of marriage, and claimed half of (what was left of) the Western Empire as her dowry.

Attila is played by the dour Jack Palance at his most sinister, and the script, not content with an Honoria in the person of the exotic French danseuse, Ludmilla Tcherina, gives him a daughter who may be the most glamorous Hun ever, Rita Gam. This Attilette is adept with weaponry, but her womanly feelings are stirred by a noble Roman officer (Jeff Chandler) who, of course, is interested in the Princess. This unlikely quadrangle comes to a thundering conclusion as Attila descends on Rome.

Fabiola: One of the movie's high points was this scene of inventive martyrdom.

BRITAIN—6TH CENTURY A.D.

In the sixth century, after the Romans had withdrawn from Britain and its politics essentially dissolved into chaos, it is thought that a minor war lord, probably named Artos, did his best to maintain civilization and Christianity in the west of England. Centuries later, the legends of his struggle were romanti-

Opposite:
Constantine and the Cross: Constantine (Cornel Wilde) sets out to conquer the Roman Empire for Christianity.

Sign of the Pagan: Attila (Jack Palance) is taken by the dancing skills of a Roman princess (Ludmilla Tcherina) in this lively piece of historical nonsense.

Knights of the Round Table: Here they all are, with table, including King Arthur (Mel Ferrer, center) and Lancelot (Robert Taylor), being lectured by Merlin (Felix Aylmer).

cized by the French and given the full panoply of a high medieval setting (in the same way that the heroes of Troy were described in terms of a much later time). Thus we have King Arthur.

Knights of the Round Table (1953) gave the Arthur story a production with full and magnificent late medieval panoply, thereby following the anachronistic lead of Malory, Tennyson et al. However, it did away with all the fantasy elements (except for that sword in the stone, or an anvil in this case), which left the audience with a fairly dull love triangle of king, queen, and knightly best friend Lancelot, in which the motives of all three were pure as the driven snow. Mel Ferrer as a put-upon Arthur and Robert Taylor a peculiarly stiff Lancelot didn't help matters, but Ava Gardner was a luscious Guinevere, and there were some splendid castles and jolly jousts. In the big battle scene between Arthur and Mordred, Arthur had obviously presciently studied the tactics of Henry V at Agincourt and the cinematographers had not so presciently studied the Olivier film of a decade earlier.

Later films on the matter of Britain were *Camelot* and *Excalibur*, both more fantasy oriented and more interesting, but there has not yet been an Arthur movie set in the correct historical period.

Opposite, above:
Knights of the Round Table: The costumes were luscious and the castles well-battlemented. Guinevere (Ava Gardner) is about to go the stake for treason.

Opposite, below:
Knights of the Round Table: The production gave the audience a never-never land Camelot of medieval legend not exactly congruent with the sixth-century Britain when Arthur was presumed to have lived. Here, treading a courtly round, are Elaine (Maureen Swanson, left), looking very much the Lily Maid, with Lancelot and Guinevere with Arthur.

The Vikings: Einar (Kirk Douglas) and the slave Eric (Tony Curtis) fight it out on a precarious perch.

BRITAIN/SCANDINAVIA—9TH CENTURY A.D.

The seventh and eighth centuries were the depth of the Dark Ages, and they were so dark that no major movie has been laid in that period. However, with fits and starts, Europe began to pull itself together. For instance, in England, the bad news was that the Scandinavian Vikings (aka the Danes), after a century of sporadic bloodthirsty raids, were invading in full force to stay. The good news was that a young "king" (of which there were many in Britain at the time) named Alfred was doing a fairly successful job of uniting all the small kingdoms against the Danes, succeeding where Arthur had failed.

The Vikings (1958) was a rousing look at Viking life, with Viking son pitted against father, and a captured Saxon princess to complicate things. Kirk Douglas was a tough, blond Viking "hero," only just a bit more civilized than his father (Ernest Borgnine), and Janet Leigh was perhaps the only American actress to achieve the British trick of making a vapid historical heroine something more than a hand-wringing ninny. What made the picture worth the price of admission, however, were the Viking settlement and ships, photographed on location in Norway. Perhaps everybody was a little more well-scrubbed than the originals, but there was the look of authenticity, and several shots of the dragon-prowed ships sweeping down the fjords in mist and rain were heart-stopping in their beauty.

Opposite:
The Vikings: The Viking Einar returns home to the fjords in his dragon-prowed boat.

Alfred the Great: Danes *vs.* Saxons in the battle that probably saved England from becoming a Scandinavian nation.

Opposite:
Alfred the Great: The movie did not magnify the pomp and circumstance of ninth-century England. This is hardly a royal entrance by Alfred (David Hemmings).

The political problems of ninth-century Britain seemed a dubious subject for a film, but *Alfred, The Great* (1969) managed to involve the viewer, nonetheless. It was an intelligently scripted biography of the young king of West Saxony who had to battle to unify the small Anglo-Saxon kingdoms in order to confront the invading Danes. David Hemmings made a good job of showing Alfred's desire for civilized values (such as learning how to read) while remaining able in war, and Prunella Ransome was a restrained and very Saxon-looking love interest. Michael York, who usually played sensitive types, did a neat reversal as a Danish warrior chief.

The film had a feel for the barely civilized culture of England in this period (no silks and satins at these courts), and meticulously staged battle scenes that conveyed a sense of reality. Everything in the production was relatively small-scaled, since everything in England at the time was small-scaled (major battles could be fought with a few hundred men). However, the memorable scene in which Alfred waits anxiously on a heath for the none-too-probable appearance of his Saxon allies, and their eventual arrival, coming from every direction, is epic in spirit if not in numbers.

Kings of the Sun: Black Eagle (Yul Brynner), war chief of his tribe, is captured by the Mayan newcomers to his land.

AMERICA—10TH CENTURY A.D.

Things were happening in other corners of the globe, too. The Mayan civilization of Central America had reached a level of sophistication beyond that of much of Europe of the time. It has been speculated on some fairly solid evidence that when their cities in Yucatán suffered invasion by barbarians, Mayan refugees escaped north across the Gulf of Mexico and influenced the Indians of the Southern United States and the Mound Builder culture.

An event of this sort was the highly original (albeit speculative) basis of *Kings of the Sun* (1963). Beginning with a vivid recreation of a Mayan ceremony filmed at a restored pyramid in Mexico, it follows a young king, Balam, and his followers as their city, Chichén Itzá, is conquered and they flee north by sea and attempt to rebuild their culture on the barren northern Gulf coast. The chief of a resident tribe is captured, and there is dissent in the Mayan community as to whether he should be sacrificed in the customary way; the young king eventually forbids sacrifice in the new land and the two peoples attempt détente (with some friction). They finally unite to defeat the original invaders of Chichén, who have followed the Mayans.

The Greek George Chakiris is an unlikely Mayan king, and the English Shirley Anne Field an even unlikelier Mayan lady (though a beautiful one). But Yul Brynner, as the local chief Black Eagle, uses his spectacular physique (of which almost all is seen—seldom has a major actor been so consistently near-naked in a film) and lithe athleticism to personify the romantic ideal of the noble savage, the heroic Indian brave of every frontier epic.

Filmed in Mexico, the movie uses the vast numbers of contemporary Mayan extras to good effect; camerawork and lighting on the more intimate scenes are often way beyond routine. The final battle, fought around and on the pyramid built by the Mayans, is as visually exciting as many in much larger-scaled films. Despite (or perhaps because of) its offbeat theme and setting, *Kings of the Sun* is handsome, colorful, and a lot of fun.

Omar Khayyam: A Persian harem in which Debra Paget (reclining) looks right at home, in this fantasia on the life of the Moslem poet-scientist. That's the exotic Peruvian singer Yma Sumac on the right.

PERSIA—11TH CENTURY A.D.

To the east and south of Europe, the conquering Moslems had absorbed and developed the ancient Persian and Egyptian cultures, and established their capital in Baghdad. At the height of this hybrid civilization, one of the most celebrated of its citizens was Abu'l-Fath Umar Khayyami ibn Ibrahim, aka Omar Khayyam. The West knows him as a poet; the East considers his poetry simply the diversion of one of the greatest of medieval mathematicians.

Omar Khayyam (1957) made the life of the poet/mathematician into a sex and sand spectacle lacking only Maria Montez. It had the usual plot of deluded Caliph and wicked vizier (was there ever a good vizier in the movies?) and included in its nefarious doings the legendary "Old Man of the Mountain," leader of the "Hashshasheen," hashish-addicted assassins. On this level it was diverting, and it was certainly gorgeously decorated, with the best use of haute Islamic sets and costumes since *The Thief of Bagdad*; Caliph Raymond Massey's throne room was a high point. John Derek as Omar looked more at home saving the kingdom than when spouting quatrains from the Rubaiyat or peering through scientific instruments (at least Omar's status as some sort of scientist was conceded). An odd bit of casting had the multi-octaved Peruvian soprano Yma Sumac as a slave girl, crooning a Persian/Incan tune at one point.

Overleaf, clockwise from above left:
El Cid: Don Rodrigo (Charlton Heston) squares off against Don Martin (Christopher Rhodes) in the best chivalric tradition.
El Cid: Charlton Heston is Rodrigo Diaz de Vivar, known as El Cid, whose part in the ongoing war between Christians and Moors in eleventh-century Spain became the stuff of legend.
El Cid: El Cid and Chimene (Sophia Loren) finally make it to the altar after the minor matter of his killing her father is cleared up.
El Cid: El Cid receives the blessing of the royal family of Castile, who are King Ferdinand I (Ralph Truman) and the Infantas, a handsome lot: Dona Urraca (Genevieve Page), Sancho (Gary Raymond, center), and Alfonso (John Fraser). Hurd Hatfield (far right) is the Herald Arias.

SPAIN—11TH CENTURY A.D.

At the other end of the domains of Islam, the Moslem Moors had occupied most of Spain for three centuries, much of which were devoted to conflict between Christian and Moslem. The mercenary warrior Rodrigo Diaz de Vivar, known as El Cid from the Arabic sayid *(noble or lord), fought on both sides, but after capturing Valencia, ruled it with justice and defended it from the Almoravid Moors. Christian Spain made him a folk hero, like Arthur, and decorated his life with many legends.*

The movie *El Cid* (1961) walks a fine line between history and legend. The young Rodrigo, on his way to his wedding, fights a battle with Spanish Moors, captures five of their Emirs, and then releases them on the condition that they will not take up arms against the Christian ruler of Spain (or more correctly, in the splintered Spain of the time, Castile, Leon, and Asturias). This is accounted treason by the conservative court, and in the resulting charges and countercharges, Rodrigo is forced to kill the king's champion, the father of his intended bride.

This causes a minor problem in the Cid's romantic life, but he and his intended are eventually married and he spends the rest of the movie attempting to unite Moslems and Christians of Spain against the common enemy, the North African Moors; in this, he is hampered by the jealousy and prejudice of the Royal Family. In the course of the film, we run through three kings of Castile and Leon; King Ferdinand is succeeded by two of the Infantas, Sancho and Alfonso. After capturing Valencia, El Cid sends the crown to Alfonso, who finally realizes that all Rodrigo desires is a united Spain and the defeat of the North Africans, who now are attacking Valencia.

Alfonso joins El Cid, who immediately succumbs to an arrow wound. Knowing that only he can rally the Spanish forces to victory, his body is tied in place onto a white horse and leads the defending forces out of besieged Valencia to victory.

This macabre and theatrical finale is the only really original touch in the movie, which otherwise moves ponderously through intrigues and battles, all well and handsomely staged but never quite alive. Rodrigo is quite simply too good to be true (especially given the historical facts), and it's to Charlton Heston's credit that he manages to make something even vaguely human out of the role. Sophia Loren as his beloved Chimene is positively kittenish in the early part of the film (and Sophia Loren being kittenish is an unnerving sight) but achieves a certain dignity and presence later.

The Royals (King Ferdinand and the three Infantas) are a handsome lot, and the set piece court ceremonial at which they are introduced (by Hurd Hatfield as the Herald Arias) has more than a touch of medieval magic about it. Genevieve Page as the poisonous female Infanta Dona Urraca, with her coils of blond hair and an insinuating viciousness, practically steals the picture; it comes alive when she's on screen. Otherwise, one must be content to watch the principals wend their two-dimensional way through a gorgeous tapestry of castles, cathedrals, and landscapes.

ENGLAND—12TH CENTURY A.D.

Our old friends the Vikings had carved out a kingdom in France and changed their name to the Normans (thus Normandy). They then conquered England, more or less by accident uniting it politically in the process. In the twelfth century the country was divided socially, however, into a mostly Norman aristocracy

Becket: Becket (Richard Burton) explains the facts of political life to the rebellious young Brother John (David Weston).

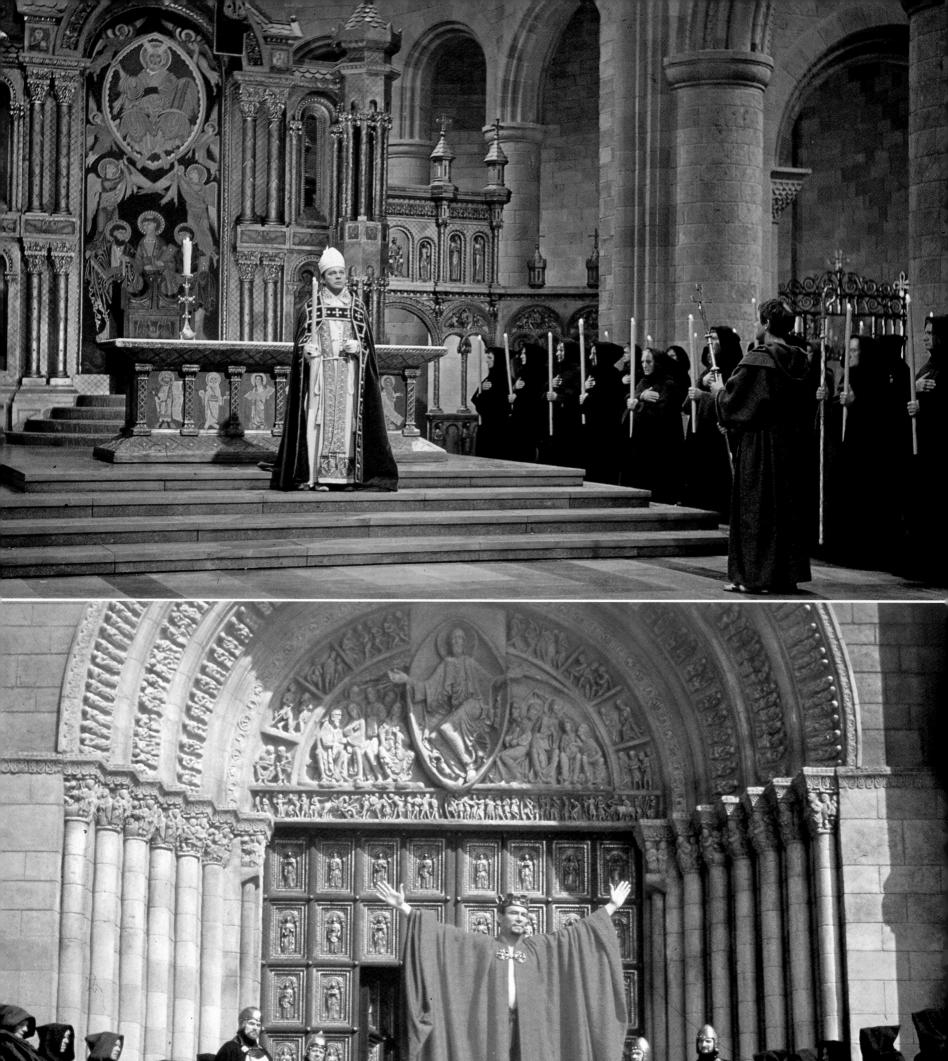

and a Saxon populace (some Saxon lords had maintained their position, as we shall see in Ivanhoe). The most colorful king after William the Conqueror was his great-grandson, Henry II, the first of the Plantagenets (through his father, Count of Anjou). He scandalized Europe by marrying an ex-queen of France (Eleanor of Aquitaine), who brought him rich French lands (a source of dispute between the two countries for the next four centuries). The most dramatic event of his reign was the murder of his friend, Thomas Becket, whom he had made the archbishop of Canterbury in order to control the Catholic Church in England. Becket, however, in an amazing volte-face, renounced his luxurious ways and became a dedicated churchman, fighting the king in every way for the rights of the Church. Henry, in an unguarded moment, expressed the wish that someone would avenge Becket's "insults" ("Will no one rid me of this meddlesome priest?" are the words traditionally ascribed). Four of his nobles, taking him at his word, put Becket to the sword at the altar at Canterbury.

Jean Anouilh's play, Becket, made a scintillating theatrical exchange of the changing relations between King Henry and Thomas Becket. The film (1964) of the play tried to keep the dramatic tension while expanding the action into a spectacle. It was mostly successful, and head and shoulders above most historical films in literacy, but was inevitably faulted by film buffs as being too talky and by theater buffs as being too gaudy.

It takes the relationship from the pair's period of brawling comraderie to the assassination of Becket, all seen as a flashback as Henry does public penance (a scourging by the clergy) for Becket's death. Much is made of the fact that Becket is a Saxon in a Norman court, and that he is a civilizing influence on the boorish Norman Henry.

Richard Burton gives one of his best performances as Becket; he makes the extraordinary turnabout from cynical courtier to Archbishop fighting for "the

Becket: Henry II (Peter O'Toole) contemplates the death site of his beloved enemy, Becket, in Canterbury Cathedral.

Opposite, above:
Becket: Becket, the playboy Saxon, has become Becket, the model Archbishop.

Opposite, below:
Becket: Henry II in robes of penitence as an admission of guilt for the death of Becket.

The Lion In Winter: Eleanor of Aquitaine (Katharine Hepburn), just out of prison, makes a stylish entrance via barge to join the family for Christmas at Chinon.

honor of God" believable. Peter O'Toole goes over the top as Henry, ranting, crying, goading, bullying; his performance is sometimes hyperactive, but perhaps it is the only way to balance Burton's calm intellectualism. Henry is a man in love and rejected ("He's never forgiven me for preferring God to him," Becket says); the entire film is the story of a love affair between two men that is everything but physical. The women are barely present; Henry's wife, Eleanor of Aquitaine (Pamela Brown), is depicted here as a shrewish prig, hardly the Eleanor of history; his mother, the formidable Queen Matilda, is equally unsympathetic. Even Becket's Saxon mistress, the beautiful Gwendolen (played with great presence by Sian Phillips, who was to be Livia in the television version of *I, Claudius*), is an object to be passed from Becket to Henry on demand.

Anouilh's light touch is evident in the portrayal of the three courts—English, French, and Papal—and their amusingly cynical intrigues as Becket seeks help from Louis VII of France and the Pope. Sir John Gielgud has never been more appealing than as the lightly malicious Louis who, despite himself, is charmed by Becket while at the same time using him.

In *Becket*, Henry says at one point that he loathes his children (four sons: Henry Jr., Richard, Geoffrey, and John), and *The Lion in Winter*, which takes place perhaps ten years later, demonstrates that he had good cause. It is set at a fictional Christmas gathering of the family at Chinon in France. Also present are the young king of France, Philip II (heir to *Becket*'s Louis VII) and his sister, Alais. The eldest son and heir, the younger Henry, has died in the meantime.

The play by James Goldman was a tour de force, a seven-player verbal tennis match in which one-liners, putdowns, and surprising revelations were lobbed about the stage at lightning speed; it was a sort of upmarket television sitcom. Every character was plotting against, conniving with, or in love with one or more of the others; the alliances kept changing with bewildering rapidity. The movie (1968) was an object lesson as to the manner in which film can slow down action, but much of the brilliance came through, and a certain amount of pageantry and an imaginative score (by John Barry) filled in the gaps. (Both contributed to the most sumptuous scene in the film, Eleanor's arrival on the royal barge.)

It was almost necessary after *Becket* that Peter O'Toole again play Henry II; this older, slightly wiser monarch was a seamless continuation of the former role. Katharine Hepburn was an Eleanor of Aquitaine to be reckoned with, aging but unbowed, and continuing to battle Henry and scheme for whichever son might suit her purpose. Anthony Hopkins was a bluff young Richard (Lionheart-to-be), interested mostly in war and (in one of the script's most startling scenes) the handsome young Philip (Timothy Dalton), with whom he has been in love since they were boys together. The other characters hold their own; the result is one of the most stimulating of historical films.

ENGLAND/PALESTINE—12TH CENTURY A.D.

With Henry II, the Plantagenets had entered history with a bang, but it was his son Richard the Lion-Hearted who really caught the public imagination for all time. In truth, Richard was good-looking (as kings went) and a great warrior. He was also boastful, impatient of statecraft, and probably homosexual (not the best of orientations for continuing the dynasty). He preferred to mount a crusade (the Third) with other European rulers rather than rule England. On the way, he married a Spanish princess, Berengaria of Navarre (for her Crusade-financing dowry, some thought). The Crusade was a good deal of sound and fury which

The Crusades: Despite the title, the movie covered only one of the Crusades (the Third), and Richard the Lion-Hearted (Henry Wilcoxon) had just the armor in which to lead it.

The Crusades: The siege of Saracen-held Acre by the Christians was a real DeMille wing-ding.

Opposite, above:
Robin Hood: Douglas Fairbanks, Sr., flying through the air as usual, in the monumental castle set for this 1922 version of the adventures of the bandit of Sherwood Forest.

Opposite, below:
The Adventures of Robin Hood: Richard the Lion-Hearted (Ian Hunter) rewards Robin (Errol Flynn), watched by Maid Marion (Olivia de Havilland) and the Merrie Men, among them Friar Tuck (Eugene Pallette), Little John (Alan Hale), and Will Scarlett (Patric Knowles).

eventually signified nothing much except the Christian occupation of Acre. Richard headed back to England, leaving poor Berengaria to live out her days in France, and all the world knows that he was captured and held for ransom by Leopold of Austria while his brother John tried to usurp the monarchy. Legends gathered around Richard's memory after he died of an arrow wound in battle, some connecting to more mythic figures such as Robin Hood.

The plurally titled *The Crusades* (1935) really only has to do with the Third; Cecil B. DeMille takes as hero Richard the Lion-Hearted, and what the movie lacks in historical veracity it more than made up for in imaginative storytelling. Richard (Henry Wilcoxon) uses the fervor of a crusading holy man as an excuse for war, and sweeps off with a motley crew of the rulers of other European countries (Germany, Russia, Sicily, Hungary) to the Holy Land to conquer its Moslem ruler, Saladin. France is represented by King Philip II and Princess Alice, the fragile Alais of *The Lion In Winter*, here in the very different guise of the sultry Katharine DeMille, the director's daughter.

There is as much rivalry and intrigue among the Christian rulers as there is fervor against the Moslems. To finance the war effort, Richard agrees to marry the daughter of King Sancho of Navarre, Berengaria, who has fallen in love with him. Since it is simply a matter of finances, he doesn't bother to attend the wedding; Berengaria symbolically weds his sword held by his minstrel, Blondel.

Disillusioned by a sword for a husband, she still accompanies Richard to Palestine. During the siege of Acre, she is captured by Saladin, who falls for her Christian charms and proves it by dressing her in jeweled harem flimsies. He is nevertheless a gentleman and not only returns her to Richard (who realizes his own love for her), but agrees to open Jerusalem to all Christians except Richard, who has vowed to lay his sword on the Holy Sepulcher. Berengaria carries it into Jerusalem in his place.

Even Cecil B. DeMille couldn't get much romantic mileage out of Richard's love life (or historical lack of same), and the central personal drama of the king and Berengaria is pretty tepid. Loretta Young, dressed in white satin robes with lots of pearls and with that particular glow that she could bring to the screen, still couldn't make Berengaria anything more than a pious ninny. The main fun of the movie was in watching DeMille stalwart Henry Wilcoxon as Richard (played very much like his Antony in the DeMille *Cleopatra*) bouncing off the subtleties of Saladin and Conrad of Montferrat (another wonderfully oleaginous performance by Joseph Schildkraut).

The siege of Acre, however, was the most enthralling such military action since that of Babylon in *Intolerance*, and the big Christian *vs.* Moslem battle scene, with the two hosts of mounted knights thundering toward each other and crashing together in a most satisfyingly bloodthirsty way, assured the audience that if DeMille hadn't stage-managed the real crusades, he should have.

The legendary Robin Hood has some little basis in fact, but his story became linked with that of John's usurpation and Richard's return from captivity. The first big Robin Hood movie was in 1922, tailor-made for the bouncy Douglas Fairbanks. It was produced by the Pickford-Fairbanks company, on whose lot sprang up a complete medieval castle, a set larger than the colossal one for *Intolerance*.

The script provided knights, archers, swords, and banners in profusion to skirmish around and inside the castle. It gave the emphasis to the Crusade and the John-Richard power struggle; Wallace Beery was not the suavest Richard, but his rough, ready, and cheerful king was a standout performance, and turned his career from villains to playing the humorous, sympathetic Beery character so familiar to filmgoers of the thirties and forties. Fairbanks careered from tree to tree and turret to turret in typical fashion, and had a jolly good time doing so, as did the audience.

An even jollier time was had in *The Adventures of Robin Hood* (1938), which has been called "the definitive swashbuckler." Errol Flynn, certainly the definitive buckler of swashes, and Claude Rains as a nasty Prince John were backed by Basil Rathbone as Sir Guy and Ian Hunter as an overly well-bred Richard. Robin's Merrie Men were headed by the rotund Eugene Pallette as Friar Tuck and the dashing Patric Knowles as Will Scarlett; his Merrie Woman, Maid Marion, was Olivia de Havilland. A rousing score and a skillful use of early color made the movie an audiovisual treat.

Richard also turns up in Sir Walter Scott's *Ivanhoe*, the story of the son of a Saxon lord who battles the bad-guy Normans (John & Co.) until the good-guy Norman (Richard) shows up, after which all settle down to become one race of Englishmen. Robin Hood (aka Robin of Locksley, as he is known here) is the leader of the Saxon underground, and he saves the day at the siege of Torquilstone castle. Also prominent in the plot complications are the Jew, Isaac of York (representing those Jews who historically financed Richard's ransom), and his beauteous daughter, the tragic heroine Rebecca. The movie *Ivanhoe* (1952) was another historical winner, with more knights, archers, swords, and banners galore and a siege to top that of *The Crusades*.

Ivanhoe: The siege of Torquilstone was the most rousing such since the Christians took Acre in *The Crusades.*

Robert Taylor's Ivanhoe is a bit sobersided and middle-aged for a dashing young knight, and Joan Fontaine struggles to make the Saxon heroine Rowena into someone who does more than stand about on the battlements wringing her hands. Both are outshone by Elizabeth Taylor at the height of her young beauty as Rebecca, whose hopeless love for Ivanhoe she imbues with just the right pathos (and emphasizes the question asked by generations of readers—how could Ivanhoe choose the boring Rowena over the fascinating Rebecca?). George Sanders and Robert Douglas also liven things up as the Norman menaces, De Bois-Guilbert and De Bracy. The impish Emlyn Williams is a delightful Wamba, the joker in the pack, and the older generation is well represented by Finlay Currie as Cedric the Saxon, Ivanhoe's feisty father, and Felix Aylmer, who makes Isaac a majestic figure indeed. (Aylmer was omnipresent in films about this period—he was Merlin in *Knights of the Round Table*, the elder Archbishop of Canterbury in *Becket*, and will be met again with the same title in *Henry V.*)

Ivanhoe very neatly walks the line between a certain realism (Cedric's banqueting hall has more than a touch of squalor) and glossy romanticism (never has a tournament looked more glamorous), and Noel Langley's script is a nearly perfect exercise in boiling down a complicated novel into manageable movie length, with some literate dialogue and faultless pacing.

CENTRAL ASIA—13TH CENTURY A.D.

Central Asia brought forth a new scourge eight hundred years after Attila's Huns. This was the Mongols, led by Genghis Khan. They devastated the Islamic countries of the Near East, a blow from which that area never recovered. On the other side of Asia, they began the conquest of China. Some few facts are known about Genghis Khan: that his real name was Temujin (Genghis Khan means "Universal Ruler"); that he was the leader of a destitute clan of the Mongols and at one point a captive and hostage of another; and that his rise to power was rapid and ruthless. He died on campaign; his successors were driven out of the West, but completed the conquest of China under Kublai Khan.

The Conqueror (1956) might well have led Genghis Khan, if he had seen it, to level Hollywood and pile the skulls of its inhabitants on Rodeo Drive. Directed by Dick Powell with apparent seriousness, it starred John Wayne as Genghis Khan, in a performance that depicted the Khan as combined cavalry captain and Indian chief. Susan Hayward, looking as twentieth-century as ever, was a Tartar (which could be considered type-casting); she makes her entrance in an ox cart. The dialogue had many great moments, but the height was probably reached when Wayne growls to Hayward, who is being a tartar—"You're beautiful in your wrath."

The Conqueror: Susan Hayward was a Tartar and John Wayne was a Mongol (Genghis Khan, in fact) in this epic foolishness. Neither was convincing.

Genghis Khan: Genghis Khan (Omar Sharif) enters the fabled country of Cathay.

The casting in *Genghis Khan* (1965) was just as unlikely: the Egyptian Omar Sharif as Temujin/Genghis; the very blond (and exquisite) Françoise Dorleac as Bortei, princess of another Mongolian tribe; Robert Morley as a sort of Gilbert-and-Sullivan emperor of China ably supported by the equally British James Mason as his chief advisor; and Irishman Stephen Boyd as the archvillain Jamuga. The casting incongruities never quite jell, and plot and dialogue don't rise above the simplistic, but somehow they aren't as ludicrous as they might be, perhaps because the movie creates a splendid never-never Mongol-land with stirring battles and magnificent landscapes (filmed in the steppes of

Opposite:

Ivanhoe: Rowena meets Rebecca. Despite the aristocratic beauty of Joan Fontaine (center), with Elizabeth Taylor as Rebecca the movie only reinforced the question asked by a century of readers—"How could Ivanhoe prefer Rowena to Rebecca?" That's Robert Taylor making the decision.

Alexander Nevsky: The battle on Lake Peipus in 1242, one of the most exciting scenes of warfare ever filmed. The Russians have the pointed helmets, the Teutonic knights are wearing the buckets.

central Yugoslavia). Costumes and sets (particularly Old Peking and the Chinese court) are as lavish as one could want, and there's even some attempt at authenticity, though the Mongols are a good deal better scrubbed than history would lead us to believe.

RUSSIA—13TH CENTURY A.D.

The Mongols, of course, invaded Russia, which was divided into many principalities in the thirteenth century. One of the greatest was Novgorod, and its most memorable prince was Alexander Nevsky, famed not for defeating the Mongols (to whom eventually Novgorod paid tribute), but for defeating the (German) Teutonic knights. This religious-military order had invaded on the declaration by Pope Gregory IX of a "crusade" against Greek Orthodox Russia.

In 1938, Nevsky's war against the Teutonic knights was a made-to-order propaganda subject for Communist Russia, since the enemy was both German and Christian. Sergei Eisenstein's *Alexander Nevsky* transcended propaganda to become a masterpiece of historical spectacle. The good people of Novgorod ask Nevsky to lead the defense against the Teutonic order, which has just conquered Pskov with attendant atrocities (Russian babies are snatched from their mother's arms and thrown into the fire).

At least a third of the film's length is devoted to the battle on Lake Peipus on that April day of 1242, and one can think of few, if any, battles that have been so exhaustively, yet clearly, re-created on film. The enemy is first seen as a

Alexander Nevsky: Nevsky (Nikolai Cherkassov) rallies the troops against the Teutonic knights.

Opposite:
Genghis Khan: Genghis (Omar Sharif) has a deadly one-on-one for the leadership of the Mongols.

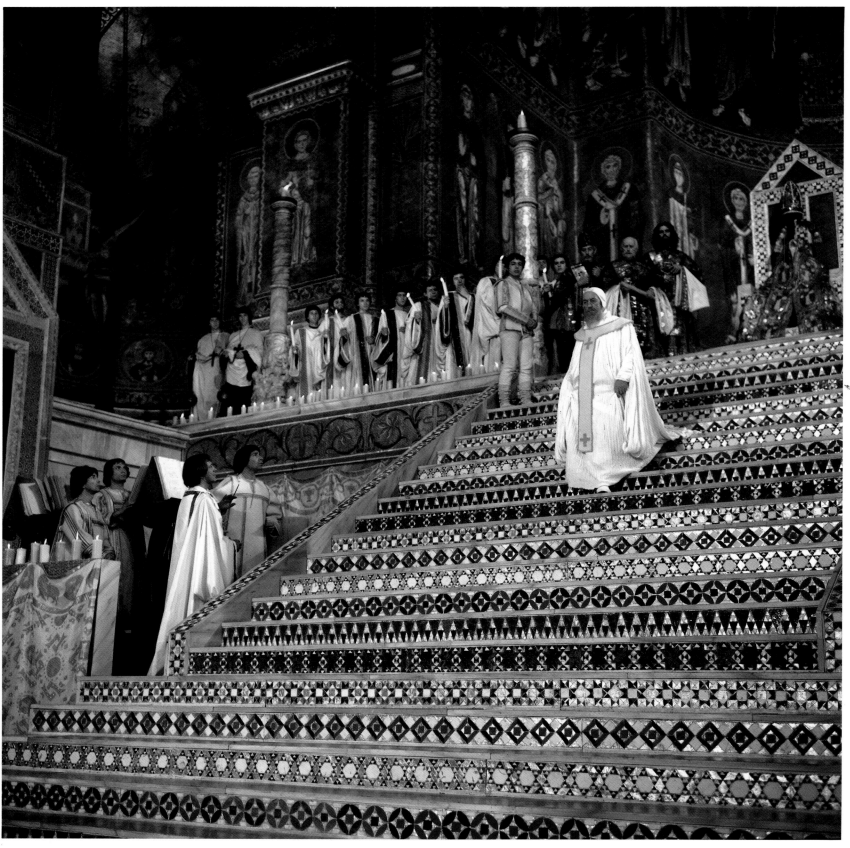

Brother Sun, Sister Moon: Pope descending a staircase. Alec Guinness is Pope Innocent III. The film emphasized the lavish Papal court of the thirteenth century as a contrast to the poverty-prone St. Francis.

force spread across the bottom of the screen, massive and yet still dwarfed by the sky above it. Battle is joined, and as Nevsky springs his trap the enemy retreats, regroups in geometric lines, retreats again until the final rout.

Through the battle, we follow the various characters we have been introduced to: Nevsky, of course; Vassili and Gamelo, the two male parts of a romantic triangle, one serious, one blustery (the woman has promised her hand to the bravest); a feisty old man; a beautiful young woman who has taken up arms.

The most immediately startling aspect of the production is the stylized costuming for the Germans—white robes (even for the horses) and bizarre helmets, bucket-shaped (making the wearers look like robots) and some with

outré devices projecting from their tops. In the final moments, the ice on the lake breaks up; as the remainder of their force is falling through the cracks and struggling in the water, the white cloaks and the ice floes become indistinguishably white-on-white.

The film is anything but subtle, and Nicolai Cherkassov is an operatically stolid hero as Nevsky. But the sheer beauty of the filming, the ongoing impetus of the battle, and, Sergei Prokofiev's monumental score, which has entered the concert repertoire, all contribute to a major cinematic experience.

ITALY/CHINA—13TH CENTURY A.D.

In Europe, the wealth and arrogance of the Roman Catholic Church was causing a reaction among the truly pious. Francesco de Bernadone ("Francesco" for his French mother) was the son of a wealthy merchant of Assisi in Italy. In his early twenties, after fighting with the Assisian army and sowing a good many wild oats, he renounced the world and began a brotherhood devoted to piety, service to the poor, and a communal ownership of any worldly possessions. The Pope, discomfited by this return to primeval Christianity, eventually gave his blessing to the community which became the Franciscans and the man who was to become St. Francis. Another Italian (Venetian, in this case) who achieved lasting renown for quite a different reason was Marco Polo, who was in effect the most famous traveling salesman in history. His mercantile family was already well-traveled: father and uncle had visited the court of Kublai Khan, successor to Genghis in China. On a second trip, they took the seventeen-year-old Marco with them; he became a favorite of the Khan, and his account of the Mongol/

*Chinese court and his travels to the Gobi desert, Java, Sumatra, Ceylon, and
other points east (the story of which was dictated to a fellow prisoner-of-war in a
Genoese jail) was disbelieved by millions of readers for centuries.*

Brother Sun, Sister Moon (1973) was a film biography of St. Francis, artfully
calculated for the audience of flower children of the time of its making. It
emphasized the peace and love aspects of Francis's hard choices, and made it
almost impossible to understand what the Catholic hierarchy could find to
object to in these sweet young people from Assisi who wanted to start a com-
mune. The film is drenched in beauty, much of it, as befits the subject, the
beauty of nature. The Umbrian hills near Assisi are beautiful. Graham Faulk-
ner (Francesco) is beautiful. The lovely, fragile Judi Bowker is the beautiful
Clare (who starts a sort of women's auxiliary to Francesco's movement). Even
the Papal court (which is apparently undergoing a Venetian period in decor) is
a knockout. It's all a bit too much beauty, but certain scenes—an endless field
of Umbrian flowers, the Pope's purple throne room—stay in the mind.

The Adventures of Marco Polo (1938) was obviously meant to be a sort of
knockabout romp built around the travels of the Venetian merchant, but a fatal
flaw was introduced with the casting of Gary Cooper as Marco. Never comfortable in any period costume save that of the American West, Cooper was one of
those quintessentially American actors whose range certainly transcended
cowboy roles, but which simply couldn't stretch to the sort of Continental
pizzazz that Colman and Flynn had naturally.

The result was a sort of "Aw-shucks" Marco traveling through a variety of
exotic landscapes, meeting Kublai Khan's daughter (Sigrid Gurie) in the conventionally cute way that cowboys meet the banker's daughter, and besting the
treacherous villain (inevitably Basil Rathbone) who wants to overthrow the
Khan. Cooper as Marco seemed but one aspect of a production determined to
Americanize Polo's adventures into a series of clichés that even a lavish production couldn't save.

112

ENGLAND/FRANCE—15TH CENTURY A.D.

The Hundred Years' War between England and France went on for over a hundred years, from the mid-fourteenth century to the mid-fifteenth; its nominal cause was the claim by the English monarchs to the French crown. Well past the halfway point, the young King Henry V of England scored a resounding victory against the French at Agincourt, using English long bows against the old-fashioned heavily armored French knights. He married a French princess, but died soon after. The French king died in the same year, and the English made such substantial gains that the French dauphin could not be properly crowned in Rheims. An adolescent girl named Jeanne appeared from the provinces, declaring that heavenly voices told her she would lead the French armies to victory. For a while, she did; the dauphin was crowned. But in a dastardly political move, she was turned over to the English and burned as a witch. The English King Henry VI was soon crowned King of France. The French recovered, eventually threw out the English, and the vacillating dauphin turned out to be something of a good king, as did his son, the eccentric but very capable Louis XI.

Several decades into the Hundred Years' War, a nineteen-year-old student decided to leave Paris, so ravaged by war that wolves come into the city at night, and walk to the coast where he hoped to get a boat for England and, once there, to study at Oxford. This is the basis for *A Walk with Love and Death,* a short, deeply affecting novel (by Hans Koningsberger) made into a small, deeply affecting film (1969) by John Huston. On the way through a land totally ravaged by war and anarchy, beset by outlaws of every class of society, the student, Heron of Foix, briefly meets Claudia, a nobleman's daughter. At Calais, about to embark for England, he hears that her estate has been ravaged by revolting peasants.

He returns and finds her in an abbey, a refugee. The two of them flee from shelter to shelter, desperately seeking to find some haven from the war. They do, briefly, but the story ends in tragedy.

This small-scaled film on one hand conveyed a strong sense of period and the attitudes and ideas of medieval France; on the other, it was one of the few films to capture the universal horror of innocents caught in the total desolation of war. Assaf Dayan, son of the former Israeli minister of defense, was a fine Heron of Foix, and the sixteen-year-old Anjelica Huston made a more-than-auspicious debut as Claudia; her unconventional good looks and special quality signaled the possibility of an interesting future career.

Shakespeare's fast and loose way with history when making it into drama set a precedent which most dramatists have followed since, and which might be interpreted as, "Don't let mere history get in the way of a good plot, a good scene, or a good line, for that matter." This, of course, also applies to filmmakers (as is more than evident from the movies cited here). And when it came to film, Shakespeare and his works became something like part of the same problem, since they themselves were history by now; if meddled with, purists screamed (in much the same way they scream when history is meddled with in a script.)

The movies had a lot of trouble with Shakespeare. On one hand, it was certainly a box-office name. On the other, well—Theda Bara miming Juliet in a silent version of the play, with snippets of the dialogue in titles, was hardly Shakespeare. And it did look a little ludicrous to have a credit on the Fairbanks-Pickford *The Taming of the Shrew* which read: "By William Shakespeare, with additional dialogue by Sam Taylor." So for the first half-century of moviemaking, there were no filmed Shakespearian plays that worked well; it was something of a surprise when they worked at all. And then Laurence Olivier made *Henry V* (1945).

This had never been considered one of Shakespeare's greatest efforts ("That's why it was a good film," say the purists). It celebrated the young King Henry's victory at the battle of Agincourt, with scenes leading up to its justifying Henry's claim to the French throne (by way of the Archbishop of Canterbury) and showing Henry rallying his men at Harfleur, their landing place in France, and quietly encouraging them on the night before the big battle. Afterwards, we see Henry gently courting the French Princess Katharine, and the agreement of the French King to their wedding.

Henry V (1944): Laurence Olivier portrayed Henry V literally as a knight on a white horse.

Olivier's imaginative approach was to open by showing us the Globe Theater in Shakespeare's time and the beginning of a performance of *Henry V*. The opening scenes, rather tedious to a modern audience, were made interesting by watching an authentically reconstructed performance as it might have appeared in Shakespeare's time. The Chorus makes his opening speech, and one remarks his crude theatrical make-up. Dear old Felix Aylmer potters about as the Archbishop of Canterbury, endlessly citing the contemporary equivalent of international law, and contending with various staging problems, the groundlings, and the venders in the audience. Subsequent scenes were set in stylized theatrical sets, but the stage of the Globe was forsaken as the action opened out into a stage that was all the world.

The Battle of Agincourt was filmed in the real out-of-doors, and suddenly reality takes over. The charge of the French knights, starting at a slow walk and very gradually building to a thundering gallop, was the most exciting thing of its kind yet filmed, and its interruption by the stunning noise of the English bowstrings and the subsequent havoc wrought by the English arrows was a sensational combination of sound and sight. After the battle, we are again in a theatrical never-never land as Henry woos Katharine. As a joyous carol rings out to celebrate the wedding, the couple appear in wedding dress; they turn to

face the camera, and we are shocked to see a roughly made-up Henry and a boy in the costume of Katharine. We are back on the stage of the Globe.

This brilliantly inventive approach to filming, combined with expert delivery of the Shakespearian dialogue by a superb cast of actors and an enthralling score by Sir William Walton, made *Henry V* not just an extraordinary achievement in cinematic Shakespeare, but an extraordinary achievement in film.

The young actor-director Kenneth Branagh came to the attention of American audiences in an unfairly neglected British miniseries, "The Fortunes of War." In it, he played an English professor abroad who insistently directed amateur Shakespearian productions in the face of the threatened Nazi invasions of Rumania and Egypt in the dark early days of World War II. There was a curious sense of *déjà vu* for those who had been impressed with his performance there when he leapt to international prominence with a new film production of *Henry V* (1989), almost a half-century after the Olivier.

Directing and starring as Henry, Branagh seemed determined to avoid any possible imitation of the earlier version, and came up with a no-frills Shakespearian movie that satisfied the purists but was accused of lacking filmic virtues. The performances, however, were a joy: Branagh as Henry, Paul Scofield as the king of France, Emma Thompson as Katharine, and Ian Holm as Fluellen were the standouts in an excellent cast.

It's a bit of a shock to realize that the noble English you're rooting for in *Henry V* are the same crowd, fifteen years later, you're rooting against in any adaptation of the Joan of Arc story. One of Cecil B. DeMille's earliest ventures into history was *Joan the Woman* (1917), made during World War I, in which a British soldier in the trenches in France discovers Joan's rusted sword and sees her career in flashback. Joan was played by the great operatic soprano Geraldine Farrar, who had a surprising success in the several movies that she made, perhaps because the acting on the operatic stage of the period was not that far from what was needed on the silent screen.

Ingrid Bergman had had a Broadway success in Maxwell Anderson's *Joan of Lorraine*; her identification with the character made it inevitable that she should play Joan on screen. A full-scale historical epic, loosely adapted from the play, was mounted around her as *Joan of Arc* (1948). It was also a full-scale disaster. Major problems were sets of stultifying artificiality, dialogue that was

Quentin Durward: This handsomely mounted film, conceived as a followup to *Ivanhoe* and also from a Scott novel, gilded the lily with skillful use of the exteriors of some of the more picturesque French châteaux.

Quentin Durward: Durward (Robert Taylor, right), a last flower on the fading branch of fifteenth-century chivalry, confronts Count Philip De Creville (Marius Goring) over a runaway heiress (Kay Kendall).

as stiff and awkward as the battle scenes, and Bergman herself. She had never been at her best when being girlish, and in no way did she convince the audience that she was an adolescent French peasant; inspiration, whether from heavenly voices or a good director, was not forthcoming.

Quentin Durward (1955), yet another adaptation from the works of Sir Walter Scott, takes place in the postwar period, and is therefore a little more lighthearted. Quentin is Robert Taylor again, as a last flower on the fading branch of knighthood (he refers to himself as an anachronism, a swordsman in the new age of guns). He is a Scots knight meshed in the schemes of the French court as he chases a lady over half of France, not for the obvious reason but to ascertain for his uncle as to her looks, breeding and, above all, her thriftiness. (Scott was not above using Scots stereotypes.) She turns out to be beautiful, brainy, and not all that thrifty (she scatters her jewels to save herself and Quentin from a band of cutthroats), and the inevitable happens in this variation on Tristan and Isolde.

A good deal less serious than *Ivanhoe*, *Durward* was equally handsomely mounted (with skillful exterior use of several of the more lavish French *châteaux*), and had the advantage of Robert Morley as Louis XI (who comes across as the only sensible character in the movie) and the brilliant English comedienne Kay Kendall as the Lady Isabelle, a most unorthodox historical heroine. Even straight-laced Mr. Taylor loosened up a little, to the extent of having a bathtub scene (nothing elaborate, mind you). Certainly the climax, a contest between Durward and De la Marck, "the beast of the Ardennes," which had the two of them dueling while swinging from the ropes of a burning bell tower, is one of the most exciting and athletic of screen battles.

Louis XI is also the eccentric monarch who turns up as *deus ex machina* in *The Hunchback of Notre Dame*. The silent version (1923) dropped most of the complexities of Victor Hugo's novel and remained a bit static despite a lavish production and an astonishing performance (and makeup job) by Lon Chaney, Sr. The remake (1939) managed a little more depth, and all the stops were pulled both in Charles Laughton's Quasimodo and the spectacular central set, medieval Paris with the cathedral of Notre Dame as its centerpiece.

Quentin Durward: Our hero ends up dueling the villain while both are hanging from the ropes of a burning bell tower, one of the more unusual movie climaxes.

The Hunchback of Notre Dame (1923): The hunchback Quasimodo (Lon Chaney), crowned the King of Fools, threatens a subject.

The Hunchback of Notre Dame (1939): All in all, this version was quite a production, both in the reconstruction of Notre Dame and the startling physical deformation achieved by Charles Laughton as the hunchback (foreground).

RENAISSANCE TO REVOLUTION

ITALY/SPAIN—15TH CENTURY A.D.

The Renaissance might seem a rowdy, bloodthirsty period to us lily-livered moderns, but after the Crusades, the Black Plague, and the Hundred Years' War, it was downright placid. Creativity and knowledge bubbled up, and after a millenium of struggle, Europe returned (or so it thought) to the level of Graeco-Roman civilization. Certainly the Borgias (originally a Spanish family transplanted to Italy) did a good job of imitating the Roman penchant for murderous intrigue, as well as having a Caesar (Cesare, in Italian) among their number. His sister, Lucrezia, did not give dangerous dinner parties; she was mostly used as a marriageable political pawn by Cesare and their father, Pope Alexander VI, and ended her days happily as the duchess of Ferrara. As a positive contrast to the Borgias, Christopher Columbus arguably made the greatest discovery of all the many discoveries of the Renaissance, a whole new hemisphere. He was an Italian transplanted to Spain, who convinced the reigning monarchs, Ferdinand and Isabella, that the goods of the Orient (highly sought-after since the Crusades) could be more easily got by sailing west. Much has been made of the trouble Columbus had in selling this (not-quite-accurate) notion, but it should be noted that the Spanish monarchs had other things on their minds as well—it was they who achieved success in a matter encountered earlier in this narrative: they drove the Moors from Spain in 1492.

The year 1949 was the year of the fifteenth century for movies; there were two about the Borgias and one devoted to Columbus. *Bride of Vengeance* wove a tale of Renaissance intrigue around Lucrezia, in the robust person of Paulette Goddard. As opposed to popular legend, here she was portrayed as a good woman, as history judges her to have been; this was less for the sake of historical accuracy than continuing the Hollywood tradition of presenting "wicked" women of history as vehicles for major female stars. Despite the wiles of brother Cesare, Lucrezia comes to love Alfonso d'Este, duke of Ferrara. Alfonso is

Opposite:
The Private Life of Henry VIII: Charles Laughton's first entrance as Henry VIII, a role that would be associated with him for decades.

Overleaf, above left:
Bride of Vengeance: Lucrezia Borgia (Paulette Goddard) and her husband, the duke of Ferrara (John Lund), dispense justice in this richly costumed Renaissance epic (a rare example of the director, in this case Mitchell Leisen, also receiving costume credit).

Overleaf, below left:
Bride of Vengeance: Cesare Borgia (Macdonald Carey looking remarkably like the portraits of the most dashing of the Borgia clan) urges sister Lucrezia to have a go with a poison ring.

Overleaf, right:
Prince of Foxes: Wanda Hendrix and Tyrone Power meet in the highest of Renaissance settings.

rather a dull fellow, mainly interested in manufacturing the world's longest
and largest cannon. But all ends well: Lucrezia gets her man, and Alfonso gets
his cannon.

Goddard, as was her wont, put her all into the role of Lucrezia, but subtlety
was not her forte. Alfonso was another stultifyingly dull role for the unlucky
John Lund (surely the symbolism of that cannon couldn't have escaped the
moviemakers). Macdonald Carey brought some life to the proceedings as Cesare, and managed to look startlingly like the extant portraits of that bravo.

Prince of Foxes is just as lively, and a good deal more edifying. Lushly
decorated and costumed (but unfortunately filmed in black-and-white), this
version of Renaissance Italy gave us Orson Welles as Cesare Borgia, looking
startlingly *unlike* the portraits, but doing a swell job of intriguing and scenery
chewing. The hero, Tyrone Power, is an artist who is also a man of action. As
Cesare's agent, he infiltrates a small city-state ruled by a dear old duke (Felix
Aylmer—who else?) with a lovely young wife. The inevitable occurs, and
Power saves the day, the kingdom, and the wife (it is, conveniently, a marriage
of convenience) after a rousing siege.

Christopher Columbus is an excellent example of the historical film that's
just too historical. There is little that is certain about Columbus's early life (we
do know of an illegitimate son by a Spanish lady named Beatriz) due to his
tendency in later years to inflate his experience and background. The script-
writers resisted the temptation to inject melodrama to liven up the film (though
Beatriz does appear). Unfortunately they also neglected to inject much drama.
The production was handsome, and Fredric March struggled valiantly to bring
some life to the cardboard Columbus role; he certainly waded ashore in the
New World with aplomb. His wife, Florence Eldridge, appeared as Queen
Isabella; again to the scriptwriters' credit, she did not pledge her jewels to
finance the expedition.

ITALY—16TH CENTURY A.D.

*The Borgia pope, the father of Lucrezia and Cesare, was succeeded by an even
unlikelier Holy Father. Julius II not only had several children, but spent a good
deal of time leading armies into battle in order to maintain (and sometimes
extend) the Papal States. He also decided to rebuild St. Peter's (the cost of which*

The Agony and the Ecstasy: This scene is apparently from the agony section, as Michelangelo (Charlton Heston) suffers the discomforts of painting the Sistine ceiling. Ecstasy is subliminally represented in the movie by his handsome apprentice.

is considered one of the major causes of the Protestant Reformation) and patronized many of the great artists of this age of great artists. One of those was Michelangelo Buonarroti, whose talent had been so evident in his youth that he had been taken into the household of the Medicis (another of those omnipresent Renaissance families) in Florence and treated as a son by Lorenzo the Magnificent. The collaboration of pope and artist was a difficult one, since both were stubborn and proud men at the top of their professions, but it resulted in the frescos of the Sistine Chapel.

The painting of the frescos is the subject of *The Agony and the Ecstasy* (1965); art and artists have seldom been well-handled in films, but this, probably because of its elephantine size, hit a new low. For over two hours, Julius (Rex Harrison) and Michelangelo (Charlton Heston) bicker over the length of time it is taking the artist to finish decorating the chapel ceiling.

This is a film with no memorable scenes, except perhaps for ludicrousness; the best of those is when Michelangelo looks into the sunrise clouds and sees the figures of God and Adam which he will eventually execute (so that's how artists get their inspiration!). Diane Cilento of the cat's eyes and purring voice (wearing Renaissance gowns superbly) drifts in and out as a Medici daughter, to whom Michelangelo keeps explaining that love and sex can't compete with his work. (Subtle hints are thrown out, however, by drawings of male nudes and an omnipresent and very handsome young apprentice.)

One is left with the impression of Harrison doing his Henry Higgins inexplicably dressed in Eliza's white gown, nattering away at poor Michelangelo, more recalcitrant by far than Eliza ever was. And how the viewer emphathizes every time Julius cries, "When will there be an end?"

SPAIN/AMERICA—16TH CENTURY A.D.

Columbus never knew that he hadn't reached Asia; that was left for Magellan, thirty years after Columbus's discovery of a New World. But even before then, it was evident that this was terra incognita, and that anything could be found there. Spaniards of all classes flocked to the small settlements that had been established in the Caribbean. Two of them struck gold. Hernando Cortes discovered the Aztec empire of Central Mexico and conquered it with an astonishingly small "army." Francisco Pizarro found the Incan Empire of northwestern South America and conquered it with an even smaller force. This was not just due to the European's superior weapons. The Aztecs, magnificent though their civilization was in many ways, were a repugnantly bloodthirsty people; their subject tribes (including the Maya) were waiting for any assistance to overthrow them. One of Cortes's chief aides was an Indian woman who became his mistress, translator, and advisor, the legendary Dona Marina. The far more benevolent Incas had built a monolithic semicommunist social system that became paralyzed if the monarchy was disabled in any way. By one of the great strokes of historical luck, Pizarro arrived there in the year of a disputed succession. The civil war had ended with the accession of Atahualpa, but the empire was greatly weakened. Pizarro captured Atahualpa, promised his release for the ransom of a roomful of gold and, that delivered, killed the Inca. The empire was his.

The hero of *Captain from Castile* (1947) is a young Spanish nobleman escaping from the Inquisition, who flees to the New World and joins Cortes's expedition. The movie made the expedition's quest into the unknown as exciting as a boys' adventure story. This was something of an accomplishment; not that many films about exciting moments of history have really been all that exciting. The

The Agony and the Ecstacy: Pope Julius II (Rex Harrison) didn't have a Popemobile, but seems well-guarded anyhow.

The Agony and the Ecstacy: Michelangelo explains to a dubious Contessina de Médicis (Diane Cilento) that love and sex must be sublimated to art.

plot is enlivened not only by the vicissitudes that the Spaniards met and overcame while trekking inland to the Aztec capital, but by the hero's continuing struggle with the long arm of the Inquisition, which has a representative along.

The movie comes to one of the most infuriating and at the same time exhilarating conclusions of any in cinema history. All crises at least temporarily resolved, Cortes calls for the expedition to break camp and move on; the goal is in sight. There is a swirl of activity, the comparatively small company of Europeans sets out on the final leg of the journey, and there is a magnificent long shot of the valley of Mexico, the great Aztec capital in the distance backed by two volcanos . . . and that's it.

Beautifully filmed on location, *Captain from Castile* takes at least basic care with historical veracity. The pyramid-templed towns on the way look right, and the Aztec dignitaries are as gorgeously befeathered as the records report them to have been. Cortes's Indian mistress is regally present. Former Latin matinee idol Cesar Romero is a cultured and virile Cortes, and Tyrone Power is a dashing protagonist. The score by Alfred Newman adds much, and is deservedly a classic.

The Pizarro expeditionary force got less sumptuous treatment in *Royal Hunt of the Sun* (1969). It was from a play by Peter Shaffer, which had been staged with a maximum of the theatrical experimentalism of the late sixties. The movie went in exactly the opposite direction, and was filmed with great realism. The core of the script in both cases is the philosophical confrontation between Pizarro and the ruling Inca, Atahualpa. Christopher Plummer had played Pizarro on stage. In a stunning turnabout, he took the role of the Inca in the film, and did a superb job, conveying a character who is the product of a totally alien culture—even the body language is quite literally something else. He was ably supported by Robert Shaw in a slightly more conventional role, though one doubts the historically crude Pizarro to have been quite so polished or articulate.

ENGLAND—16TH CENTURY A.D.

The Tudors, particularly Henry VIII and Elizabeth I, lived such intensely dramatic lives, both emotionally and politically, that they have become the legendary royalty, and variations and interpretations of what is known about them (which is quite a bit) have been legion. Henry inherited the throne as a young man and seemed the true Renaissance prince—he was actually educated, he composed music and wrote verse, he was able in statecraft, and he was handsome to boot.

And like the Renaissance itself, his reign was anything but dull, and it changed the course of his country forever. As the world knows, he went through six wives. Their names are confusingly repetitive—Catherine (of Aragon), Anne (Boleyn), Jane (Seymour), Anne (of Cleves), Catherine (Howard), Catherine (Paar). Their fates are equally repetitive—divorced, beheaded, died of natural causes, divorced, beheaded, died of natural causes (the last after Henry's death).

All this left three royal offspring and the country itself divorced from the (until then) omnipotent Catholic Church, which Henry fought in another battle of Church and State. In this, he and Thomas More repeated, in a different key, the tragic story of an earlier Henry and Thomas.

Henry's three children all ruled, though the two girls had on and off been declared bastards. First, of course, in a male-dominated society, was the young Edward VI (son of wife number three) who died at fifteen. Then Mary (daughter of wife number one and granddaughter of Ferdinand and Isabella) was queen for five years. And then it was the turn of Elizabeth (child of wife number two).

Top:
Captain from Castile: Tyrone Power in the title role is a member of Cortes's conquering expedition into the empire of the Aztecs.

Above:
Royal Hunt of the Sun: Two totally alien cultures meet as Francisco Pizarro (Robert Shaw) tries to communicate with the Inca Atahualpa (Christopher Plummer).

This virile queen reigned for forty-five years, brought England to the status of a world-class nation, and never married. There has been speculation that there was some sort of physical impediment to matrimony (even, by extremists, that she was really a male), but one need only to look at her father's marital history to see that from her point of view the acquisition of a consort was absolute folly, for the kingdom and herself. Her assumption of the role of the "Virgin Queen" was, unfortunately, more than a little undermined by a succession of male favorites such as Sir Walter Raleigh and the Earl of Essex, even though there is no absolute proof of physical intimacy with any of them. But she seemed as ready as her father to behead those she had loved. Other Tudors, such as Henry's sister Mary and her granddaughter Jane Grey, have also entered legend.

The Private Life of Henry VIII (1933) was the first British film to be a major hit in the United States. For a generation the image of Charles Laughton as a corpulent Henry, lustily gnawing on a capon and throwing the bones over his shoulder, was irrevocably set in the public mind. It was a stylish and somewhat artificial movie; the succession of wives was rather like a series of music hall turns. (It starts with number two—Catherine of Aragon was ignored as too dull.) At least four of the "wives" made enough of an international impression

The Sword and the Rose: The Sword (Richard Todd, right) saves the Rose (Glynis Johns) from the Duke (Michael Gough).

The Sword and the Rose: An early Tudor measure is trod by Mary (Glynis Johns), sister of Henry VIII, and the commoner Charles Brandon (Richard Todd), whom she would eventually marry after her brief stint as the queen of France.

Opposite:
Anne of the Thousand Days: A for Anne (Genevieve Bujold), H for Henry (Richard Burton). King meets girl, king gets girl—after upsetting all of Christendom.

to eventually go to Hollywood: the beautiful Merle Oberon (Anne Boleyn); the pretty Wendy Barrie (Jane Seymour); the very funny Mrs. Laughton, Elsa Lanchester (Anne of Cleves); and the energetic Binnie Barnes (Catherine Howard). Lanchester in particular was a delight as the extremely Germanic Anne, whom Henry loathed at first sight.

An early Mary Tudor, Henry's younger sister, was less well-known than Henry's daughter, but her life was as hectic and dramatic as any Tudor could wish. It was chronicled in *The Sword and the Rose* (1953). Mary was the Rose; the Sword was presumably Charles Brandon, born a commoner and created Duke of Suffolk. Mary actually became Queen of France—for three months—having been married off at age sixteen to the aging Louis XII by brother Henry. In swashbuckling style, the movie tells how Brandon comes to France after King Louis dies to save his true love Mary from some slimy French intrigue or, worse, from becoming the only adolescent Queen Mother of France on record. Glynis Johns and Richard Todd are a romantically handsome pair in this ro-

mantically handsome movie, and James Robertson Justice is a satisfyingly bombastic Henry.

Anne Boleyn and her tempestuous relationship with Henry VIII is the sole concern of *Anne of the Thousand Days* (1969), based on the play by Maxwell Anderson. Historical opinion is still divided as to whether Anne was an ambitious schemer who got in beyond her depth or a silly girl totally unmindful of what she was doing. Anderson's script gives yet another motivation for her actions and is a splendid example of how historical facts can be reinterpreted with a minimum of distortion for a maximum of dramatic effect.

Here the king's fancy settles on Anne just after she has returned from a stay at the French Court, and she is in the throes of first love with Henry Percy, future Earl of Northumberland. King Henry is finishing an affair with Anne's older sister, Mary, leaving her with child and not much else, though the family continues to be in high favor with the king. Percy is forced to marry elsewhere, and Anne, bitterly angry at the interference and mindful of her sister's abandonment, tells the king, along with some well-chosen insults *re* his music and verse, that she will only bed with him as his wife, no matter what he does to her or her family. (As Henry is already married, this is to Anne an utter impossibility.) She loathes Cardinal Wolsey, who has acted as pander for the king, and has nothing but contempt for Henry.

Her insults intrigue the king even further, since no one has naysaid him for years. His passion for Anne grows as her resistance holds, and this provides the tinder for the smoldering resentment of Queen Catherine for not bearing a son.

To Anne's utter amazement, Henry (almost literally) moves Earth and Heaven to divorce Catherine, and finally does so. By this time, Anne has grown to love him, and after their marriage and her coronation, they are happy. But it seems that Henry is one of those people whose interest in an acquisition lasts in inverse ratio to the effort expended in getting it. He soon tires of Anne, and this is exacerbated by the birth of first a daughter (Elizabeth) and then a dead son. At Henry's instigation, his favorite advisor, Thomas Cromwell, invents evidence of Anne's adultery, with her brother and a court musician among others, and she is brought to trial for high treason, convicted, and beheaded. (During her imprisonment, she enumerates to herself the "thousand days" since she has succumbed to the king.)

While some viewers felt that the movie should have been titled *Anne for a Thousand Days* (it is a long film), it is probably the most cracklingly dramatic of all the Tudor movies. Most of the credit for this must go to Geneviève Bujold, who is on screen for most of its length and who delivers an astonishing performance. With her flag of auburn hair, she is truly delectable in the early scenes; she actually makes the bulky Tudor costumes alluring. And she pulls a trick that until then has seemed the exclusive province of Vivien Leigh; she grows from girl to woman before our eyes.

Richard Burton gives her solid support as Henry; this is the most humanly believable of all the Henry portrayals. He is not quite a monster in his royal selfishness, and is transparent in his self-delusion of always doing the right thing. Irene Papas, sallow, sad, and greasy-haired, is a pathetic Catherine of Aragon; she allows her fire to show through only in a brief appearance before the court set to judge the legality of her marriage. The movie is handsomely set, and for once pageant and drama are balanced in one neat package.

The much honored *A Man for All Seasons* (1966; six Academy Awards) is indeed an achievement in intelligent moviemaking. It follows Sir Thomas More in his conflict with the king, replaying in a very different mode the basic conflict of king and Becket. More is a State Councilor when the film opens, and

A Man for All Seasons: Henry VIII (Robert Shaw) presents Sir Thomas More (Paul Scofield) with the knotty problem of divorcing Queen Catherine.

A Man for All Seasons: Sir Thomas More on trial for not condoning the divorce.

A Man for All Seasons: Vanessa Redgrave made a cameo appearance as Anne Boleyn, newly married to Henry.

Young Bess: Princess Elizabeth Tudor (Jean Simmons) is accused of treason by the Lord Protector (John Carradine), the brother of Henry VIII's third wife (above). Below, she is watched over by Thomas Seymour (Stewart Granger), another brother of her father's third wife and the future husband of his widow (Tudor geneology gets complicated).

the Chancellor of England, Cardinal Wolsey, is deeply embroiled in the question of the king's divorce from Queen Catherine. When Wolsey dies, More becomes Chancellor, avoids committing himself on the issue, and eventually resigns. But he will not sign the Act of Succession which in effect makes Henry head of the Church in England (and therefore able to grant himself a divorce). Confined to the Tower of London for two months, he is tried and convicted by perjury on the part of a minion of Thomas Cromwell, who has continually been shown as More's chief nemesis. The film ends with More's execution on the block.

Throughout, we are shown More as a very human man in a multitude of scenes with his family at their home in Chelsea. Henry appears in only one extended scene, where he pays an "impromptu" visit to the Mores, trailed by boatloads of courtiers. And More's primary strategy is made clear—as a lawyer, he knows that in law, silence is assumed to mean consent, so if he remains silent on the issue of the king's divorce, he will be safe.

Nevertheless, literate though the script is, not much life shows through. Sir Thomas is made to appear the only upright man in England, with everyone else caving in to the king, who is a jovial, temperamental monster. But More's strategies begin to smack of sophistry, since their point is not to speak out on this issue about which he feels deeply enough to eventually lay down his life. The film's thesis boils down to a complex issue reduced to black-and-white simplicity and then presented with a veneer of complexity. Paul Scofield, as

More, creates a likable and intelligent character who eventually becomes something of a bore in his single-mindedness. Robert Shaw's Henry is loud and handsome (Henry was still relatively young and thin at the time). Wendy Hiller and Susannah York are More's loving, shrewish wife and knowing daughter, characters on a more human level than the principals. Vanessa Redgrave makes a cameo appearance as Anne Boleyn, with no dialogue but still vividly conveying the impression of a lustful, conniving adventuress.

Young Bess (1953) deals with the young womanhood of Elizabeth, in dramatic if somewhat spurious terms. It would have it that the adolescent Elizabeth was smitten with Thomas Seymour, brother to the protector, Edward Seymour, and uncle of the young successor, Edward VI. Contrary to history, which looks upon Thomas as an ambitious schemer, here he is a dashing visionary, deeply in love with Henry's widow, Catherine Paar, whom he eventually marries. This romantic triangle is complicated by the ceaseless power struggles surrounding the child king and the princess (older sister Mary is hardly mentioned), who is in and out of favor depending on how the political winds are blowing. The story proceeds as a flashback (on the day of Elizabeth's assumption of the crown) from the last days of Henry's reign to the execution of Thomas Seymour for conspiracy to gain the throne by marrying Elizabeth, a conspiracy of which neither of the major parties is guilty in this version.

This romantic claptrap was vastly enhanced by some very handsome sets and costumes, some wit in the telling (Elizabeth's stubborn refusal to give in to her father) and an amazing cast. The major players were four of the British cinema's finest gifts to the American: the inimitable Charles Laughton, reprising his Henry; Jean Simmons, allowed to show some temperament as well as beauty, as Elizabeth; Deborah Kerr, another intelligent beauty, as Catherine Paar; and Stewart Granger at his swashbuckling best as Thomas Seymour. This brilliant assemblage, supported by some fine English character actors, made it all almost believable.

Anne Boleyn had a thousand days; poor Jane Grey only had nine. The sad story of the "Nine Days' Queen" is told in *Lady Jane* (1985): how this granddaughter of Henry's sister, after the death of the young Edward VI, became Queen through the machinations of the Lord Protector (to whose son she just happened to be married), and how, with no other backing, she was arrested after nine days and eventually beheaded. There is tremendous pathos in the story; Jane was just sixteen at the time and didn't want to be queen. After

Lady Jane: Lady Jane (Helena Bonham Carter) marries Guildford (Cary Elwes), the son of the ambitious Lord Dudley who would raise her to Queen for nine days. History says she was an unwilling bride; the film made it into an eventual love match.

Lady Jane: After reigning for nine days, the young Jane Grey is beheaded as a rival to Mary Tudor.

La Reine Elizabeth (Queen Elizabeth): Sarah
Bernhardt saw this film as "my one chance of
immortality." It was probably the first attempt
at what might be called the "art film."

Opposite, below:
The Private Lives of Elizabeth and Essex: The
study of the love-hate relationship between two
strong personalities, Queen Elizabeth I (Bette
Davis) and the Earl of Essex (Errol Flynn).
Here Essex makes an entrance, looking glum.

Opposite, below:
The Private Lives of Elizabeth and Essex: Here
Elizabeth makes an entrance, looking grim.

Queen Mary's accession, Jane asked, "May I go home now?" The movie presents the story with a minimum of melodramatic adornment and a maximum of
historical veracity; the results are a bit chill dramatically, but illuminating as
to an odd corner of the Tudor saga.

Sarah Bernhardt's only film was *La Reine Elisabeth* (1912); recognizing the
movies' potential, she was eager to do it as "my one chance at immortality."
Produced in France, it was arguably the first *succès d'estime* of the cinema, and
also a huge hit in Europe and the United States.

Later Bette Davis practically cornered the market as Elizabeth I for two
decades as Charles Laughton had done as Henry VIII and in something of the
same way, by a full-blown performance that rattled the rafters and left an
indelible impression in moviegoers' minds. This was in *The Private Lives of
Elizabeth and Essex* (1939, aka *Elizabeth, the Queen*), again from a play by
Maxwell Anderson.

Though the movie makes concessions to the medium with some action,
specifically the campaign Essex waged against Tyrone in Ireland, the heart of
the film is three extended scenes between the two principals in which they run
the gamut from screaming rages to tenderness, and which are in essence dis-
cussions on the matters of love, pride, and power expressed in the most
dramatic of terms. The balancing act between emotion and ambition for these
two proud individuals is brilliantly sustained by Davis and, of all people, Errol
Flynn, who held up his end of the unequal contest very creditably.

Davis reprised the role in *The Virgin Queen* (1955) and the script reprised
the love/hate situation, this time around with an earlier favorite, Sir Walter
Raleigh, who had the temerity to secretly marry one of Elizabeth's ladies in

waiting. But the dialogue lacked pith, the Raleigh lacked stature (the capable, handsome and short Richard Todd just didn't fill the screen as Flynn did), and, in all, it seemed much ado about nothing (e.g., the lady in waiting who is played by a pre-Dynastic Joan Collins).

SCOTLAND—16TH CENTURY A.D.

Mary, Queen of Scots, was a Stuart, but her life was as dramatic as any Tudor's and was, in fact, entwined with the Tudor dynasty. She inherited the throne of Scotland when she was less than a week old. Married to the Dauphin of France, she became Queen of France at seventeen. He died after two years as king; she returned to rule Scotland having been in France for thirteen years, a French-woman in everything save her father's lineage. But since that lineage included Henry VII of England, she was next in line to the English throne after Henry VIII's children, which made those children, especially Elizabeth, more than a little suspicious of her.

Queen Mary married a countryman, Lord Darnley; gossip soon had it that he wanted to be queen, with an equal lust for power and for David Rizzio, Mary's court musician and confidant. To compound confusion, Rizzio was reputed to be the father of Mary's son, the future James I of England. Darnley, with some friends, killed Rizzio in Mary's presence; he in turn died suspiciously, perhaps at the instigation of the Earl of Bothwell, to whom Mary had turned for support. The support extended to marrying her, and the God-fearing Calvinists of Scot-land had had enough of these carryings-on. They forced her abdication in favor of her son, and she escaped to England, where she threw herself on the dubious mercies of Elizabeth. This lady kept Mary in captivity while deciding whether to behead her or not. After nineteen years of dithering, she did so.

Mary's operatically emotional life was romanticized by generations of adoles-cent females into high tragedy, a view that reached its epitome in *Mary of Scotland* (1936, from yet another play by Maxwell Anderson, who seemed determined to present the entire sixteenth century on the Broadway stage). It starred Katharine Hepburn as Mary; this was in her "box office poison" days, and one can see why—what a fluttering of eyelids and mannering of speech! The high-falutin' dialogue became even higher-falutin' from her lips; Hepburn seemed determined to out-queen Bette Davis in her own way.

Opposite:
The Virgin Queen: Bette Davis reprised her memorable Elizabeth I for this unmemorable movie. She's seen here in a cozy moment with Raleigh (Richard Todd) and in a less cozy moment when he's imprisoned in the Tower of London.

Mary of Scotland: Katharine Hepburn as Mary, Queen of Scots, goes to the beheading block with all due pomp and circumstance.

Overleaf, left:
Mary of Scotland: Hepburn played Mary as the tragic, romantic heroine of generations of adolescent schoolgirls.

Overleaf, above right:
Mary, Queen of Scots: Glenda Jackson was Elizabeth I. She became as identified with the character as had Bette Davis.

Overleaf, below right:
Mary, Queen of Scots: Vanessa Redgrave, as Mary, Queen of Scots, arrives in Scotland from France with some misgivings.

Mary was shown as always acting from the best of motives, whether they be the good of the people or the search for true love, which she found in the arms of dependable Fredric March as a kilted Bothwell. Any sexual innuendo was missing, aside from the pearls on Danley's pantaloons. This was made doubly certain by the casting of the cadaverous John Carradine as Rizzio; a stylish actor, in no way could he be envisioned as anyone's object of lust. Elizabeth, in the person of Florence Eldridge, was played as a preview of Margaret Hamilton as the Wicked Witch of the West. The film is endless, and by the time we get to the final trial scene, photographed in a stylized manner with the judges in a sort of balcony wa-a-a-a-y up there and Mary in a sort of arena wa-a-a-a-y down there, all one can hope for is a beheading as soon as possible.

On the other hand, *Mary, Queen of Scots* (1971), in the later style of historical verismo, showed Mary's headstrong life, warts and all. She was embodied in Vanessa Redgrave, looking wartlessly beautiful (as Mary was reputed to have been). Compared to the earlier film, the script took few liberties with fact (though incorporating as such some of the more scandalous allegations), but by some miracle Redgrave made Mary, in all her emotional silliness, a good deal more sympathetic than had Hepburn. It used the Scottish landscape of moors, lochs, and castles to excellent effect, and a strong supporting cast including Timothy Dalton (the 007 of the late eighties) as a believably ambivalent Darnley, Ian Holm an Italian Renaissance Rizzio, and Patrick McGoohan a strong, silent Bothwell. Though supposedly Mary and Elizabeth never met face-to-face, both films have them doing so. The later film has the enormous advantage of Glenda Jackson repeating her Elizabeth (from television's "Masterpiece Theatre") in what would almost have been a cameo role for anyone else, and the screen crackles when she and Redgrave have their rencontre.

FRANCE—16TH CENTURY A.D.

The father of Mary Stuart's short-lived French husband was Henry II of France; his mother, the Italian Catherine de Médicis (a descendant of Lorenzo the Magnificent). This royal pair was two sides of a durable triangle; Henry's mistress, Diane de Poitiers, who was twenty years his elder, lasted out his reign (and ten children by his wife). She set the pattern for the royal French mistresses such as Madame du Pompadour who all but ran the kingdom, and did so with a good deal of common sense.

When Henry was killed in a tournament, Diane retired to her estates, and Catherine became the power behind the throne, ruling through her three sons who became successive kings. Obviously this family had problems. The eldest (Francis II) married Mary Stuart and died young. The next (Charles IX) was slightly unstable and, in the chaos of the French religious wars of Catholic and Protestant, gave the order that resulted in the St. Bartholomew's Day massacre in which thousands of Protestants were killed. The third (Henry III) reigned fifteen years, confused the court with his transvestitism, and outlived his powerful mother by only a few months. With him, the Valois dynasty ended.

On the face of it, *Diane* (1956) would seem another of those star vehicles featuring great women of history and in the process whitewashing them into heroines. It is that, and takes considerable liberties with Diane de Poitiers's biography in the process (not the least of which is her age—Lana Turner was in no way going to be twenty years older than her leading man). But given this cinematic license, the script by Christopher Isherwood creates an interestingly dramatic situation in the triangle of Diane, Henry, and Catherine de Médicis.

Mary, Queen of Scots: Mary (Vanessa Redgrave) is greeted by her people also with some misgivings.

Diane: Diane (Lana Turner) teaches the
awkward young prince (Roger Moore) to fence.

Diane is, of course, given the best of motives; the awkward young Henry is
put into her care by his father to polish for his marriage of state to Catherine.
Catherine and her Italian courtiers are represented as a sort of Medici Trojan
Horse, placed in the French court by Catherine's uncles to rule France in their
best interests. Diane and Henry fall in love; Henry does his duty and marries
Catherine, who also falls in love with him (and is unaware of the lengths to
which her uncles' wicked henchmen will go).

The Medici minions are responsible for the death of Henry's older brother,
the dauphin; Henry becomes king, and establishes a sort of cozy *château à
trois*. Only three of Catherine's ten children are shown, presumably the three
kings-to-be; they call Diane "Auntie." Mary of Scotland doesn't show up at all,
though she was at the French court during the latter part of Henry's reign.
Eventually, when Henry follows Diane's anti-Medici advice, the Italian fac-
tion places a defective lance in the weapons rack during a tournament. Henry
is pierced in the eye through his helmet and dies, leaving Catherine in effective control of France. There is a final confrontation between the two women;
they guardedly admit that they loved the same man, and Diane bows out of
politics.

This romantic interpretation is beautifully produced; sets and costumes are dazzling (though the royal guards' particolor uniforms have a certain musical-comedy air about them). Turner matches the decor in dazzle, and Marisa Pavan belies her fragile appearance by giving a strong performance as Catherine, dressed in ribbed bodices that make her appear skeletally sinister. The very young Roger Moore is splendid as Henry, making the difficult transition (with the help of a wide variety of facial hair) from lumpen adolescent princeling to an every-inch-a-king monarch.

One of the four ongoing narratives in D. W. Griffith's *Intolerance* (1916) has to do with the later career of Catherine de Médicis. "The Medieval Story" is less well-developed than the Babylonian or modern episodes, and the relative obscurity of its period made it the least popular of the four. It has to do with a lovely Huguenot lass (Margery Wilson), unfortunately given the soubriquet "Brown Eyes" as was Griffith's wont with his heroines (Mae Marsh, in the modern sequence, is "The Dear One"). Brown Eyes, her family, and her suitor (Eugene Pallette, the rotund character actor of many later films) meet their deaths in the St. Bartholomew's Day massacre. This is shown to be the responsibility of Catherine, now at the height of her power with her second son, Charles IX, as king. Catherine is played by Josephine Crowell, a lady whose formidable girth made Marie Dressler look sylphlike. Charles's throne room is magnificent, with the Unicorn Tapestries adorning the walls echoed by unicorn candelabra hanging from the ceiling. The massacre scenes, in Paris streets illuminated by a full moon, are among the innovative wonders of this great film.

RUSSIA—16TH CENTURY A.D.

Ivan the Terrible, Part 1: Ivan (Nikolai Cherkassov, looking far different from his role as Alexander Nevsky) intimidates a member of his court.

Opposite, above:
Ivan the Terrible, Part 2: The Polish court, at least in contrast to the Russian, is very civilized indeed.

Opposite, below:
Ivan the Terrible, Part 2: Ivan (Nikolai Cherkassov) finds that the Russian throne is not a comfortable one.

To the east, the strange and exotic country of Russia was getting itself together, mostly through the conquests of the Grand Princes of Moscow; Ivan III adopted the title czar (Caesar). His grandson Ivan IV inherited the throne at age three. Neglected by the court and buffeted by power struggles, he was to become Ivan "the Terrible," seizing power at age thirteen. The first of his many wives was Anastasia Romanov, whose family was to become the ruling dynasty ended by the Russian Revolution. Though the last part of Ivan's fifty-year rule was marred by acts of cruelty (mostly perpetrated in his periodic fits of insane rage), the major aims of his reign were laudable, at least from the Russian point of view: to extend Russia to the south to the Black Sea (which meant conquering the Moslem Khanates) and to the west to the Baltic (blocked by Livonia, whose Teutonic knights had been defeated by Alexander Nevsky), and to break the power of the boyars (the nobility). In the latter cause, he made a major grandstand play in mid-reign; he "resigned," took his family and court, and moved to his summer home. The people demanded his return; he did and, with this mandate, totally remade the power structure of the country.

Let's face it, Sergei Eisenstein's monumental two-part film, *Ivan the Terrible,* is something of a chore for modern Western audiences. The stagy acting and slow, posed direction seems a regression from the comparatively more active *Alexander Nevsky* (and the prints circulating in the United States, with mostly white-on-white subtitles, don't help). Part I (1945) takes Ivan from his coronation to the recall from "retirement"; on the way, we get his wedding feast, the siege of Kazan (the eastern front), reports of defeat by the German-Livonians (the western front), and the ongoing struggle with the boyars, represented by Ivan's Aunt Efrosinia and her effete son, Prince Vladimir, whom she wants to be Czar.

The wedding feast is particularly busy: amidst the hundreds of stuffed swans and jeweled goblets, there is an invasion of the palace by the peasants, a view of the burning suburbs of Moscow, and an arrogant demand by the Kazan Khanate for tribute. The siege of Kazan captures a bit of the old Nevsky action, but there are still many static shots of Ivan artfully posed against the lavish tents of his army. The walls of the city are blown up with a satisfyingly large explosion (but it's not noted that it was a German engineer who supervised the sapping). And as for the intrigue on the home front, what skulkings and scuttlings and lurkings in corners, what shadowy silhouettes on walls and peerings over shoulders, close-ups held for minutes with only the eyeballs rolling or an eyebrow lifted for yet another pregnant look!

Inevitably, given the Stalinist milieu in which Eisenstein was working, there are historical distortions. One, inexplicably, is that Ivan IV was the first of the Moscow princes to rule Russia. He is presented as something of a hero (albeit a broody and temperamental one). Anastasia (Ludmila Tselikovkaya) is depicted as an exquisite and saintly woman always dressed in white, and her poisoning by Aunt Efrosinia a tragedy, an odd view of the first major Romanov. Nikolai Cherkasov's makeup as Ivan is pretty peculiar; he's given a head shape pointed obliquely upwards, and a thin beard pointed obliquely downwards, and the end effect is something like a human pickaxe.

Part II (1958), subtitled *The Boyars' Plot,* is mostly about palace intrigues, though there's an early sequence in the overdecorated court of King Sigsamund of Poland, who seems to have discovered rococo before the French. Otherwise, Aunt Efrosinia is still skulking about the palace, and Ivan, though close to being convinced of her guilt in Anastasia's death, vacillates about

condemning a member of his family (like Elizabeth *re* Mary Stuart). Finally, during a tumultuous banquet suddenly in color and replete with much hearty Russian folk dancing and singing, Ivan dresses the drunken Vladimir (who pathetically confesses he doesn't want to be Czar) in Ivan's royal robes, knowing that there will be an assassination attempt. The ruse succeeds, Vladimir is killed, and Ivan concludes with a chauvinistic speech with a remarkably modern political ring to it.

Part I had been a great hit, but Part II, finished in 1946, was so disliked by Stalin that it was not publically shown until five years after his death. A third film had been planned, but was not produced because of Eisenstein's death. Though much of the two extant films appears ludicrous or opaque to modern eyes, it should be noted that they were made for a totally unsophisticated audience of an almost alien culture; they were in their ways as stylized as grand opera or kabuki theater. When viewed as such, there is much that is fascinating and visually stimulating to be found in them.

FRANCE—17TH CENTURY A.D.

You'd think Henry IV of France would have known better when starting a new dynasty after Catherine de Médicis' brood had finished off the old one. But no— he married Marie de Médicis who, on his death, decided to run things. If possible, she was even more heavy-handed than Catherine; the only matter in which she was an improvement is that her son, Louis XIII, turned out rather well. He had the good sense to rely on his chief minister of state, Cardinal Richelieu, who was, on the whole, a governmental genius. (He's been criticized for caring more for France than for the French people, but you can't have everything.) When it came to a showdown between Maman and the Cardinal, Louis chose the Cardinal, and Marie decamped to Brussels, where she set up a court in exile. Louis's queen was Anne of Austria; since Louis was homosexual, she led a rather dull life, so a little credence might be given to that old gossip, La Rochefoucauld, who implied some sort of romantic interest between her and the Duke of Buckingham, the Englishman who was at the time wielding a great deal of power across the channel under Elizabeth I's successor, James I, son of Mary Stuart.

Viewers of the many screen versions of Alexander Dumas's *The Three Musketeers* usually end up with two questions. One is, considering the amount of swordplay involved, why are they called *musketeers?* The other is, what with all the brouhaha revolving around the queen's jewels, *which* queen are we talking about? To answer the first question, firearms (i.e. muskets) were still a new invention, mostly used in battle; personal combat was kept gentlemanly with swords. As for the other, we have two clues—one is that the villain of the piece is Richelieu, the other is that the jewels in question were a love token to the Duke of Buckingham. Yes, it's poor Queen Anne.

The Three Musketeers is the story of a country bumpkin from Gascony, one D'Artagnan, who comes to Paris determined to become one of the king's musketeers, regarded as a sort of elite glamour corps. With the help of a string of unlikely coincidences and an excellent dueling technique, he does so, falling in with the three most dashing of the company, boon companions all (". . . for one and . . . "). In the process, he is smitten with the beautiful Constance, a lady-in-waiting to the queen, and becomes involved in a court intrigue having to do with some diamond studs, a present from Louis to Anne that she has unwisely given to Buckingham. In the background is the ominous figure of Richelieu, hoping to bring about the queen's downfall for his own nefarious ends, and his agent, "Milady" (de Winter), a glamorous aristocrat with no morals whatsoever.

There have been more like three hundred musketeers than three in film, given innumerable versions of the novel as well as sequels, spinoffs, and spoofs. The first big version was another Douglas Fairbanks superproduction (1921), with himself, of course, as D'Artagnan. The results, needless to say, were athletic and spectacular. There was a production in 1935 that was lavish, but curiously middle-aged with character actor Walter Abel as D'Artagnan and the dignified Paul Lukas as Athos.

In 1948 there appeared a very lively version that, given the studio (MGM), cast, and period, looked more like a musical than a drama. This was not necessarily to its discredit; the high production values given musicals then made for a ravishing production. Gene Kelly was as gymnastic a D'Artagnan as Fairbanks, June Allyson was both pert and sweetly vulnerable as Constance, and Lana Turner made a glamorous Milady.

If the 1948 edition seemed a musical without songs, the one made in 1974 was a slapstick comedy with class. Richard Lester, who had brought his jokey

The Three Musketeers (1921): Douglas Fairbanks, Sr. (second from right) was the D'Artagnan in this silent version of the Dumas novel.

The Three Musketeers (1921): Fairbanks spent much of his time as D'Artagnan, as usual, in the air.

The Three Musketeers (1948): Milady de Winter (Lana Turner) begs for mercy to the satisfaction of Athos (Van Heflin), watched by Porthos (Gig Young) and D'Artagnan (Gene Kelly) in this colorful version.

The Three Musketeers (1973): Richard Lester's jokey direction brought new life to the hoary classic, aided no end by the talent of the Three plus one: Porthos (Frank Finlay), Athos (Oliver Reed), D'Artagnan (Michael York), and Aramis (Richard Chamberlain).

directorial talents to the first two Beatles films, came up with a first-rate romp with wonderfully inventive scenes such as a wholesale duel in a laundry, with all the perils of hanging sheets and spilled soap. The entire cast carried the gags and the thrills with distinction: Michael York was both sexy and funny as hero and clown D'Artagnan; Raquel Welch displayed comedic talents as well as her more well-known ones as Constance; Milady Faye Dunaway was the best archvillainess since the Wicked Queen in *Snow White*; Charlton Heston, of all people, didn't have many jokes but showed enormous presence as Richelieu; and Oliver Reed led the Three as Athos with a lot of panache. (A sequel, with the same cast and actually made at the same time, was called *The Fourth Musketeer*).

ENGLAND—17TH CENTURY A.D.

England, so far, had escaped the religious wars that were embroiling all Europe, mainly because of Henry VIII's major and decisive break with Rome. But there were more and more Protestants of various sects (notably the Puritans) for whom the Church of England was not satisfactory, and near the middle of the seventeenth century, civil war broke out against Mary Stuart's grandson, Charles I. Religion was only one of the reasons; class, economics, and Charles's high-handedness were also significant contributors. This civil war has long been the source of many a romantic legend; never has an internal struggle been so (superficially) clear-cut. On one side were the gallant Royalist Cavaliers, with their plumed hats, elegant costumes, and flowing locks, to whose cause flocked sympathizers from all of Europe, such as Charles's nephew, the dashing Prince Rupert of the Rhine. On the other were the dour Protestants, soberly garbed and with the soup-bowl haircuts that were to give them the name Roundheads. They were led by Oliver Cromwell, a small landowner and a distant kinsman of Henry VIII's henchman, Thomas Cromwell. Alas (temporarily) for romance—Cromwell turned out to be a mighty general, both in strategy and in disciplining his Puritan forces into an irresistible fighting machine. He captured the king, beheaded him, and won the war.

England was declared a Commonwealth, and for over a decade Cromwell ruled as Lord Protector. On his death, his son took over for a brief period, then resigned. The beheaded king's son was crowned as Charles II; this Restoration monarchy, as if to make up for years of Puritan rule, became one of the merriest and most licentious in English history.

Cromwell (1970) is an impeccable historical movie, beautifully and accurately produced, with a fine mix of battle sequences and dramatic political maneuvering. It might better be called *Charles and Oliver*, since it cuts constantly between the two antagonists, beginning with Cromwell and the recall of Parliament in 1640, and includes the battles of Edge Hill, the first of the war and disastrous for the Roundheads, and Naseby, in which Cromwell's troops proved themselves against overwhelming odds. It goes on though Charles's arrest, trial, and conviction (for conspiring with foreign powers) and gives a powerful view of the horror which even the Puritans felt at regicide. The movie effectively ends at the king's beheading, though there is a final brief section concerning Cromwell's reluctant rise to Lord Protector.

The script does a fine job of condensing the complicated issues into drama without distorting them. It does, though, have a point of view: much is made of Cromwell, the champion of the rights of the common man, and perhaps too little of the religious fanatic that he is thought by some to have been. In fact, the religious issue is underplayed; only a scene or two enlighten us as to the

Puritans' anger at Charles's Catholic queen, Henrietta Marie (Dorothy Tutin), or the "Popish practices" that were introduced into English churches. And there is little sense of the great tragedy of the broader issues of the war, that of families and friends divided by a hate-filled conflict which the United States would discover two centuries later in *its* Civil War.

Richard Harris is a fine Cromwell, making human a character that has not been given many dimensions by history. Alec Guinness is Charles, presented by the script with the several conflicting portraits of the monarch that have come down to us—arrogant autocrat, stammering and indecisive leader, loving father and husband, noble victim. Even if they all don't quite jell, scene by scene Guinness is superb. Timothy Dalton is every romantic's Cavalier prince as Rupert of the Rhine, thirsting for battle and shamed by defeat. The sets are sumptuous, particularly the recreation of Parliament House, and the battle scenes have the rare quality of making a spectator feel actually present at an historical event.

And then there was *Forever Amber* (1947) which seemed to match its rowdy Restoration period as the austere *Cromwell* matched its. Kathleen Winsor's novel shocked the nation with its story of a Puritan girl who bedded her way to the top of Restoration England. Amber was a scarlet Scarlett, without that lady's vague nods to propriety by at least marrying the men she wanted to use. Amber made her way from cutpurse to highwayman's moll to kept woman to king's mistress in the raucous stews, brothels, theaters, and mansions of Restoration London, and on the way survived multiple childbirths, Newgate prison, the Great Fire of London, the accompanying plague, and all those spaniels that King Charles II had ever on hand. It, of course, had to be a movie. On the other hand, in those days of strict film censorship, how *could* it be a movie? And who was to play Amber?—a burning question which in its day was almost as important as who was to have played Scarlett a decade before.

It *did* become a movie; the two questions were answered with a bowdlerized script that still managed to be somewhat racy (Amber was limited to one illegitimate child) and with Linda Darnell. This brunette beauty did her worldly wise best with the role, but blond curls didn't really become her. Cornel Wilde wasn't much helped by *his* Cavalier hairdo either, but was stalwart as Amber's true love. George Sanders was everything Charles II should have been (including spaniels). The production was a Restoration spectacular indeed, and the excitement of duels, plague, and the Great Fire certainly made up for a lack of steaminess.

ENGLAND/AMERICA—17TH CENTURY A.D.

The civil war in England was a major contributor to the colonization of English North America. Even before, numbers of religious dissenters had fled England; the best known were the group that chartered the ship Mayflower *in 1621 and after a harrowing voyage, established a successful colony in Massachusetts. Thanks to Longfellow, several of its members have gone down in American mythology—the carpenter, John Alden; the Puritan maid, Priscilla Mullins; and the experienced mercenary, Miles Standish. The Puritans and other various Protestant sects settled mostly in the northern colonies; the South attracted the aristocrats, such as some of the great Catholic families who were also suffering religious persecution from the Church of England. (The American Civil War was in a way a replay of the English, with the Protestant North against an aristocratic South.)*

Opposite, above:
Forever Amber: Amber, the Puritan girl, has definitely made it to the top, with the not disinterested help of Charles II (George Sanders).

Opposite, below:
Forever Amber: Amber (Linda Darnell) goes against the tide of refugees from the Great Fire of London to the rescue of her lover.

Cromwell: Alec Guinness was the image of Charles I, at least as Van Dyke pictured him.

Cromwell: Richard Harris was a suitably dour Cromwell, leading his invincible Puritan fighting machine in England's civil war.

Plymouth Adventure: The Mayflower braves a storm en route to America in this re-creation of the initial voyage of the Pilgrim Fathers (and Mothers).

Plymouth Adventure (1952) might well have been titled *Plymouth Disaster.* Purporting to tell the story of the voyage of the *Mayflower* from Plymouth to Plymouth Rock in 1620, it presented the viewer with a cast of well-groomed Hollywood actors pretending to be seventeenth-century religious dissenters, who even after months at sea have spotless linen and shining, beautifully coiffed hair (even the men). There are, of course, a few sailors on hand as well—since they are presented as villains (always grumbling and begrudging their drinking water), they're allowed a little more dishevelment. Their captain, however, is invariably well-barbered, though he's a sea-going knave who does nothing but revile the passengers and make their lives even more uncomfortable than need be for months in a ninety-foot-long wooden boat. He conceives a passion for the beautiful wife of William Bradford who, for completely mystifying reasons, returns the feeling. Caught between the two men, she conveniently (and ambiguously) falls overboard and drowns while the *Mayflower* is anchored off the Massachusetts shore. This event turns the Captain pro-Puritan, and, despite the sailors' wishes, he keeps the *Mayflower* on hand through the winter, for providing comfort and care to the settlers.

This balderdash is presented against the most spurious series of sets seen since the early silents. Process seascapes and painted sunsets abound, though a storm at sea in the middle of the voyage attempts some realism and manages to raise a little excitement. (Even wet and seasick, however, the actors still manage to look remarkably unbedraggled.)

An excellent cast tried valiantly to bring some life to these American folk heroes. Van Johnson was a contentious John Alden, always fighting with the sailors (but not Miles Standish, with whom it was no contest for the vapid Priscilla Mullins of Dawn Addams—Standish is represented as married). Gene Tierney was certainly the most glamorous Puritan ever as Mrs. Bradford. The usually unsinkable Spencer Tracy's Captain Jones was a two-dimensional character—one dimension in the first part of the film, another dimension in the second.

GERMANY—17TH CENTURY A.D.

In Europe, the religious wars continued. Particularly horrendous was the Thirty Years' War, an infinitely complex struggle between Catholic and Protestant states, especially the German—Germany-to-be was at the time divided into hundreds of independent principalities. The larger nations intervened and manipulated, mainly Sweden and France attempting to fulfill Richelieu's grand schemes. It left most of that part of Europe which would be Germany almost totally devastated.

In the later part of the century, a personal drama that would affect history played itself out in one German state. Sophia Dorothea, a minor German noblewoman, married George, the son of another Sophia, the Electress of Hanover. After bearing him two children, a boy and a girl, she was accused of adultery with an aristocratic Swedish soldier of fortune, divorced, and imprisoned for thirty-two years until her death. This would have been the most minor of scandalous footnotes to history if the Electress Sophia had not been a great-grandaughter of Mary Stuart. When the last of the Stuart rulers of England, Queen Anne, died with none of her many children surviving, the throne of England went to Sophia's son, who became George I of England. The unfortunate Dorothea's son became George II, her daughter the Queen of Prussia.

The Last Valley (1971) takes place in a sparsely inhabited valley deep in the Alps which is literally the only place for hundreds of miles that has not been

The Last Valley: A band of mercenaries
descends into a peaceful Swiss valley during
the Thirty Years' War.

The Last Valley: Michael Caine is the captain of
the mercenaries, an embittered German soldier
of fortune.

Saraband for Dead Lovers: A high point of the film is Sophia's search for her lover through a surrealist street festival.

Saraband for Dead Lovers: Sophia Dorothea (Joan Greenwood, center right) is not happy with her husband, the future George I of England (Peter Bull, center left).

devastated by the Thirty Years' War. A scholar from Heidelberg, fleeing a band of looting mercenaries, comes upon the valley and is followed by the soldiers. The scholar, Vogel, arranges a sort of truce—the villagers will feed and shelter the troop for the winter (and provide women for them), and in return, the mercenaries will not pillage and will protect the valley and its inhabitants from other invaders.

The film follows the events of the winter and the relationships that develop between the soldiers, brutalized by decades of war, and the peaceful peasants. There is religious friction—the peasants are Catholic, with a fire-breathing, conservative priest; many of the soldiers are Protestant. In particular, there is the peculiar entente that grows up between Vogel and the captain of the soldiery, a precise, educated professional reduced to total cynicism by the war. This curious accord is rendered the more poignant when they discover that the captain took part in the destruction of Magdeburg, in which Vogel's wife and family had been killed.

A soldier, fleeing the penalty (castration) for rape, escapes the valley and returns with others to sack it—they are ambushed and killed by the captain and his men in concert with the villagers. When Spring comes, the captain departs despite the pleas of Erica, a woman who loves him, and Vogel. The villagers are also capable of violence; Erica is tortured and burned as a witch. The captain returns, mortally wounded, to die; Vogel, always the outsider, leaves the valley.

This quite surprising movie is a study in contrasts. It is breathtakingly beautiful (filmed in a spectacular valley in the Tyrol), very violent (but no more so than the era it portrays), and has a script of more than a little intelligence, particularly in the exchanges between Vogel and the captain. In the latter role, Michael Caine (with the slightest of German accents) is practically perfect.

Another oddity is *Saraband For Dead Lovers* (1948) which was a product of that exuberant postwar period of English filmmaking that gave us *Caesar and Cleopatra*. It is equally lavish in its telling of the story of poor Sophia Dorothea, who might have been queen of England had she not strayed. She is played by a very young Joan Greenwood, before she had got purring down to an art, and George of Hanover is played by Peter Bull, that most porcine of actors. So it's easy enough to see how her eye might wander to the dashing Swede Konigsmark in the person of Stewart Granger. When George demands yet another son (she's given him two children already), she attempts to flee with her Swedish

lover. They are caught, he is killed, and she is imprisoned. This is played out against the endless intriguing of the Hanovers to obtain the British throne (that's why a second son was wanted—it would have been a plus), led by George's dragon mother, Sophia, played to the hilt by the great French actress, Françoise Rosay.

The film's high points are the performance of Flora Robson as the aging Countess Clara, Konigsmark's mistress, and the search by Dorothea for Konigsmark through a German "Mardi Gras," a street festival thronged with masked revelers and dominated by a Lord of Misrule, a baroque sequence anticipating the surrealist sequences of *The Red Shoes.*

Saraband For Dead Lovers was unique for its time in its relative objectivity—there was no attempt to justify its heroine and glamorize her into "a good woman" (as in the Norma Shearer *Marie Antoinette*, for instance). The historical circumstances were enough to speak for themselves. In its way, this forgotten but lavish film might be considered the first of the modern historical dramas.

SWEDEN/ITALY—17TH CENTURY A.D.

Another strange personal drama played itself out in Sweden in midcentury. Sweden had became a major (Protestant) power, and its queen, Christina, was a woman of formidable intellect and culture, particularly interested in philosophy. She had been on the throne since she was a child (her father had been killed in the Thirty Years' War) and had shocked Europe by her adoption of masculine dress and manners, a declaration of freedom from the established female role of the time that only a queen could get away with. Even more shocking was her abdication at age twenty-eight in favor of her cousin, prompted primarily by her wish to convert to Catholicism, a move not allowed by the laws of Sweden. She traveled the courts of Europe, made her home in Rome, and eventually established a salon in Rome that became one of the intellectual lights of the age.

Christina seemed a role that Greta Garbo was destined to play, and she played it to the hilt in *Queen Christina* (1933). The film is probably the epitome of the romanticization of history. Here Christina, out on her own dressed as a man, takes refuge in an inn where she meets a tall, dark stranger who turns out to be

the Spanish Ambassador on his way to her court. Her gender revealed, but not her identity, there are several nights of passion (they're snowed in). She decides to abdicate for love (the religious question is touched on so slightly as to be nonexistent), but just after she does, her lover is killed in a duel. The famous final shot shows her aboard ship leaving Sweden (the wind blowing the sails one way, her hair another).

This historical nonsense makes a splendid tear-jerker of a movie and, on its terms, is gorgeously produced. In the central scene, between the queen and the ambassador in the firelit lodgings of the inn, the camera follows Garbo as she moves about the room ("I have been memorizing this room. In the future, in memory, I shall live a great deal in this room"—a line subtly linked only by the score to the scene in which her lover dies in her arms). It's probably the most romantically erotic scene in screen history. Garbo's often overdone moodiness fits the character of the melancholy lady; for once, the accent of a foreign-born star is right; and she looks great in the male Cavalier fashions of the day ("I shall die a bachelor," Christina says). John Gilbert, who Garbo demanded be her co-star for personal reasons, is a good deal more adequate than his unfortunate reputation in talkies would have it.

Exactly forty years after *Queen Christina*, there was *The Abdication* (1973) which acts as a sort of postscript answering the question, "Whatever became of the ex-queen of Sweden?" It has a striking opening—the abdication ceremony itself, lit by hundreds of candles. After that, things go somewhat downhill, as Christina (Liv Ullmann) goes to Rome. Her conversion being of the utmost political importance in this time of religious struggle, she is given one Cardinal Azollino (Peter Finch) to examine her faith. Again poor Christina, who in

reality spent her life determinedly uninvolved in any sort of emotional entanglement, is seen struggling with romantic passion, this time with a man of the cloth. There is a great deal of talk about emotional and spiritual matters, and not, unfortunately, much action in either direction.

RUSSIA—18TH CENTURY A.D.

In the first half of the eighteenth century, another queen established herself as a legend. Catherine II of Russia, unlike Christina, wanted power, took it, and held it. A minor Prussian princess, she married Peter the Great's grandson, who came to the throne as Peter III. He was a thoroughly unstable type (generally thought to have been a little weak-witted, possibly due to his adult propensity for playing with toy soldiers) and the royal pair was totally incompatible. In a coup, Catherine deposed him and assumed the title of Empress. He was soon assassinated; Catherine swore she didn't know a thing about it. She ruled still-primitive Russia with an iron hand, extended its boundaries, and, again unlike Christina, pursued sex consistently (one of her favorites became king of Poland). However, if she had been as persistent in her debaucheries as rumor would have it, she'd never had time to be as strong a ruler as she was.

Catherine has been consistently presented in the movies as yet one more noble woman forced into her actions for the good of herself and her country, another example of the popular cinema determinedly making heroines of strong historical ladies of dubious morality (not that it hasn't done the same thing often enough on the male side). The first major film about Catherine took this to an extreme. *Catherine the Great* (1934) starred the twittery Elisabeth Bergner who, like her fellow Austrian, Luise Rainer, seemed to specialize in cooing and sobbing. Her early scenes as a German princess in the barbaric Russian

court were played more like Marie Antoinette than a believable Catherine, and the casting of the matinee idol Douglas Fairbanks, Jr., as Peter redoubled the farcical quality. The movie is slightly redeemed by a sumptuous production (though again more Versailles than St. Petersburg) and the ever redoubtable Flora Robson as the Empress Elizabeth, Peter's formidable aunt.

You'd never guess that Josef von Sternberg's *The Scarlet Empress* (1934), which appeared in the same year, was about the same woman. The script also

Catherine the Great: Young Catherine (Elisabeth Bergner) marries Peter (Douglas Fairbanks, Jr.), heir to the Russian throne.

Opposite, above:
The Scarlet Empress: Catherine, having deposed her husband in a *coup d'état*, is carried on the shoulders of her supporters toward greatness.

Opposite, below:
The Scarlet Empress: The decor for this biography of Catherine the Great was weird and wonderful. The relatively human head is that of Marlene Dietrich as the young Princess Catherine.

A Royal Scandal: Although in a lighter vein, Tallulah Bankhead was as glamorous a Catherine the Great as Dietrich, and a good deal funnier than Bergner. Here she enjoys a toast from her current sex object, William Eythe.

provided Catherine with endless justifications, but with Marlene Dietrich playing the role one has the feeling that even without them she would have seized the throne, if only to appear in the white hussar's uniform she dons at the climax. A Tristan and Isolde theme is introduced early; Count Alexei, the Russian Ambassador Extraordinary sent to fetch Catherine from Prussia, is indeed extraordinary, the sexually compelling John Lodge, perhaps the only actor pre-1960 to look good in shoulder length hair. He is a decided contrast to her intended bridegroom, Peter, who is a disheveled cuckoo portrayed with relish by Sam Jaffe; certainly getting rid of *this* can only be good for the country.

Disillusionment brought on by Peter's halfwitted hostility and the discovery that Alexei is lover to the Empress Elizabeth impels Catherine into her wicked, wicked ways; no bones is made in this film about her early promiscuity. She bears a child that is obviously not Peter's, but nevertheless she is established as the mother of the heir. When Elizabeth dies, Peter makes it clear that she will be sent to a nunnery so that he can marry his sultry mistress (played by the beautiful Ruthelma Stevens). This impels Catherine to appeal to the army (most of which, it is implied, have at this point shared her bed); they rise and declare her sole ruler. Peter is strangled in his chapel by Catherine's latest lover.

Von Sternberg's films, particularly those with Dietrich, are famed for their baroque sets and photography, but the byzantine milieu of *The Scarlet Empress* gave him the excuse to go over the top. Almost no scene in the film is without surprise, visual or dramatic. The wedding scene is astonishing. The undefined space is packed with a mosaic of priests, candles, icons, and royalty; this crowded screen alternates with closeups of Dietrich's face, framed by a Russian headdress of pearls, a candle held close to her lips wavering with her breath. This Imperial Palace would never be mistaken for Versailles: every room is dominated by monumental statuary in primitive Russian style; every door is twelve feet high, and even the handles must be reached for; every chair is backed by a grotesque carving larger than life and the Imperial throne is an enormous eagle. And at the climax of the movie, Catherine (in the white hussar's uniform) enters the palace on a white horse at the head of her mounted cavalry, thundering up the great stairs and into the throne room.

Those seeking historical veracity won't find it in *The Scarlet Empress*, but it is perhaps the greatest example of a film that takes an historical theme and weaves from it a startling work of art. The only wrong note is the score, a mishmash of Mendelssohn, Wagner, and Tchaikovsky. It's the sort of classical potpourri a silent film pianist would have improvised.

A rather different Catherine was provided in *A Royal Scandal* (1945) by none other than Tallulah Bankhead. This sophisticated and hilarious film revolved around an incident in which, for once, the royal eye was cast on the wrong person, a naive but slavishly loyal young man who looked superb in a uniform (William Eythe). He has ridden hundreds of miles to report a plot of which Her Majesty is perfectly knowledgeable. Bankhead's attempts to seduce this dunce while maintaining her dignity, under the watchful eye of her chief minister (Charles Coburn), the French Ambassador (Vincent Price), and the dunce's fiancée, a lady-in-waiting (Anne Baxter), provide a perfect vehicle for Bankhead's comic talents. The dialogue is sparkling, and it's worth the price of admission simply to watch Bankhead's expression whenever she is referred to as "Mother of All the Russias."

AMERICA—18TH CENTURY A.D.

The Americas had now been filling up with Europeans for two centuries and were beginning to develop from colonial appendages to cultures in their own right. Exploration continued, however, in the enormous spaces of the two continents. The Spanish conquistadores still lived on in Mexico, sending expeditions to the unexplored Pacific coast of North America, such as the one Fra Junipero Serra, a Franciscan, accompanied. As ever, the schizophrenic mission was to search for gold and convert the Indians, but Fra Junipero stayed to become a champion of the native Americans. Inevitably, the French of the Northeast and the English of the lower Atlantic coast collided, resulting in the French and Indian Wars. Indians fought on both sides, but preferred the French, who seemed more interested in trapping and trade than settling in and taking over, as did the English colonists. In addition to making Canada British (with a huge indigenous French population), these wars taught the colonials their own military strength and gave their leaders invaluable practice in warfare in the American wilderness, a very different thing from war as waged in Europe.

This came in handy when the English colonies below Canada revolted against England. The immediate miracle was that these thirteen ministates could combine, and it took world-class minds, such as Thomas Jefferson's, to bring this about. France, smarting from her loss in Canada, gave the colonies a lot of help, and they succeeded in their bid for independence. This little war, fought in another hemisphere, was watched with great interest by opponents of monarchy in Europe.

Seven Cities of Gold: Father Junipero Serra (Michael Rennie), known to history for his concern with Native Americans, has his first encounter with them led by the well-decorated Jeffrey Hunter (right).

Opposite:
Northwest Passage: "Roger's Rangers," New England militia in the French and Indian Wars, on a punitive expedition to Canada.

Seven Cities of Gold (1955) purported to tell the story of the expedition from Mexico that brought Father Junipero Serra to Northern California. The expedition is led by tough conquistadore Richard Egan (who looked about as Spanish as he did Persian in *Esther and the King*), a good deal more interested in the fabled Seven Cities of Gold than in converting and/or helping the natives. But of course Father Junipero (the imposing Michael Rennie) shows him the error of his ways, aided by such noble savages as the talented Rita Moreno (ever fated to be cast in films as exotics with names such as Ula) and Jeffrey Hunter.

Northwest Passage (1940) is the somewhat fictionalized version of an incident in the career of Robert Rogers and his rangers (a colonial American guerrilla band), a punitive expedition into Canada during the French and Indian Wars against a French fort on the St. Francis River. It's given the tired device of the rite-of-passage induction into military discipline of the effete young tyro, Harvard graduate and artist Langdon Towne, taken along by Rogers because he needs a mapmaker. (As played by Robert Young, Towne seems no tougher at the end than he was at the beginning.) Nevertheless, it's a remarkably detailed and realistic view of colonial warfare. The large force of rangers slogs through swamps, sleeps in trees, fords vicious rivers, and leaves behind their wounded comrades to die. The attack on the French fort *cum* Indian village is shown from beginning to end—from the incursion at dawn by five rangers to the final slaughter of the surviving Indians—as one extended scene, and it's something of a tour de force. (This has drawn criticism as a distasteful depiction of brutality against native Americans from contemporary critics who ignore the fact that the colonial wars were savage affairs with atrocities committed by both sides.)

Unconquered: Why Boris Karloff, as Guyasuta, chief of the Senacas, looks so glum is a mystery, since his warriors seem to have Gary Cooper just where they want him.

The trip back from Canada becomes an exercise in survival; the troop of rangers has no supplies and almost starves in the early autumn forests of New England until they finally reach the point where the British army has agreed to meet them. Rogers as scripted is a near superhuman martinet; as played by Spencer Tracy at his bluff best, he becomes almost believable. Despite the fact that it's a slightly too well-scrubbed colonial America, the movie is a taut and exciting excursion into historical filmmaking.

(*Northwest Passage*, by the way, is something of a misnomer. It usually refers to the sea passage early explorers hoped to find at the top of the North American continent. Here Rogers dreams of finding a Northwest passage by land, which was to be the theme of a sequel that was never filmed.)

Cecil B. DeMille had always been interested in the American frontier (he filmed *The Squaw Man* three times); in *Unconquered* (1947) he just went back a way, to the time when the Western frontier happened to be in Pennsylvania. The setting is just after the French and Indian wars—the French have bowed out, but the Indians have gone on the warpath against the British all along the frontier. Whether it's Indians *vs.* British or Romans *vs.* Christians, though, DeMille gets in his bathtub scene—here it's Paulette Goddard bathing in rustic splendor in the world's largest oaken bucket, with Gary Cooper as her knight in buckskin pouring water over her head. She is an escaped bond slave,

he is a Virginia gentleman heeding the adventurous call of the West. He rescues her from the clutches of brutal redskins; in the process they narrowly escape going over the falls in a canoe. The climax of the film is the siege of Fort Pitt (Pittsburgh to be), and its relief by Cooper and assorted British troops.

Here for the first time we come upon DeMille's ambiguous attitude toward the American Indian. Many movies, from the silents on, had portrayed the Native American, kindly if not necessarily accurately, as the noble savage; there had even been hard-hitting social statements from the studios about organized exploitation on the reservations (such as the unfortunately titled *Massacre* in 1934). DeMille's pet property, the above mentioned *Squaw Man*, was a powerful plea for tolerance. But in his later films, the Indian was often portrayed as a bloodthirsty barbarian. One wonders if the casting in *Unconquered* of Boris Karloff as the Seneca chief Guyasuta was for his acting ability or because of his horror-film reputation. Whichever, Karloff did an admirable job. Cooper was as at home in buckskins as he was in a ten-gallon hat, and Goddard was her usual spirited self. The movie as a whole is enjoyable nonstop action *cum* DeMille hokum; what's lacking is the often sly wit that characterized so many of his thirties movies. Ponderousness was setting in.

Probably the most engaging of the colonial American movies is *Drums Along the Mohawk* (1939). It is John Ford's first film in color, and very simply follows the lives of a young couple who move from the well-settled coastal colonies up the Hudson to the Mohawk valley to join other settlers who are determined to tame the wilderness and make a new life. That life is far from dull, even after the forest is cleared and soil is tilled. There are attacks by Indians in the frontier uprising, and then the young husband is called to the Revolution, from which he returns wounded.

Drums Along the Mohawk: Henry Fonda (center) conquers the wilderness with a little help from his frontier friends.

Drums Along the Mohawk: The Indians take exception to their wilderness being conquered and have at the settlers, among them Ward Bond on the left.

While Claudette Colbert's dresses may be too well laundered and the home interiors too perfectly decorated in American colonial, as one major critic complained, the film still gives a wonderful vision of life on the eighteenth-century frontier. Much is made of the hospitality and helpfulness of the earlier settlers to the newcomers, and a colorful lot they are, led by the indomitable Edna Mae Oliver as a widow running her own homestead. There is an unforgettable scene in which her farm is attacked by Indians; her bedroom is invaded by Indian braves, whom she coerces by sheer Oliverian fortitude into carrying her precious four-poster bed (with herself in it) from the burning house.

Ex-Cleopatra Colbert makes a trim pioneer housewife; there are the usual little jokes about the gently bred woman confronting the booby traps of rural life (which she would replay just as amusingly in a contemporary mode ten years later in *The Egg and I*). Henry Fonda is inevitably the ideal American colonial husbandman. The climactic scene, in which the local militia, tattered and decimated, return in a pouring rain from the war (of which we only see the home front, as it were), is harrowing, as the young wife searches the sodden line of men passing her door for her husband. Ford may only have been showing us idealized American mythology; if so, would that it were always this well done.

The Howards of Virginia (1940) replays much of the plot of *Drums Along the Mohawk* in a slightly different key (moving it to the southern frontier) and

on a broader canvas. Cary Grant is the young surveyor who takes his aristocratic wife into the wild West (of Virginia—the Shenandoah Valley). The movie attempts the epic by covering two generations, and family conflict is woven into national conflict during the Revolution. In this one we do get scenes of the war, as well as glimpses of Washington, Jefferson, and other notables. Some footage was shot at the then–newly restored Williamsburg, and the general effect is that of an elaborate July 4 pageant, with Grant looking fiercely uncomfortable in buckskins.

John Paul Jones (1959) would seem to be the only movie biography of any of the great men of the American Revolution, and with that as an example, the others might well be thankful. Despite Robert Stack striving mightily to be shipshape as Jones and cameo appearances by Bette Davis as Catherine the Great and Charles Coburn as Ben Franklin, this tedious epic sank without a trace.

The box office returns on *Revolution* (1985) would seem to prove that the moviegoing public did not want the Revolution demythologized, or at least not in the way this film went about it. It centers on an Adirondack frontiersman, Tom Dobb (Al Pacino), who comes to New York and gets caught up in the war for independence, and it goes about telling the story with the new realism,

Opposite, above:
The Howards of Virginia: Howard (Cary Grant) and his aristocratic wife (Martha Scott) take a fling on the frontier (the Shenandoah Valley).

Opposite, below:
The Howards of Virginia: An elegantly dressed Thomas Jefferson (Richard Carlson) shares a bad moment with the Howards.

175

John Paul Jones: Catherine the Great (Bette Davis) gives Jones (Robert Stack) a geography lesson in Russian.

determinedly avoiding the romanticizing that went into any of the older historical effects (see any of the above). The end product was a colonial America seemingly populated by characters from the 1980s, with Marxist and Freudian overtones and lots of gratuitous violence (Dobb's young son is tortured by a sadistic redcoat officer, among other things.)

ENGLAND/POLYNESIA—18TH CENTURY A.D.

Exploration continued, and an incident in the Pacific, which occurred between the two revolutions that shook the world, entered legend. The crew of a small ship of the British Navy, which had sailed to Tahiti to pick up breadfruit as an experimental crop for the British West Indies, mutinied against a tyrannical captain. This captain was put to sea in a small boat in the vastness of the South Pacific and managed to make it to the coast of South America. The mutineers returned to Tahiti, took women aboard, and settled on an isolated island called Pitcairn. The ship was the Bounty, *the captain was William Bligh, and the leader of the mutineers was named Fletcher Christian.*

Opposite:
Revolution: Americans look back on their revolution as more dignified than the French, but perhaps the fervor was equally colorful.

176

Mutiny on the Bounty (1935): Fletcher Christian (Clark Gable, foreground left) and Captain Bligh (Charles Laughton, right), 1935 version.

This story was first told on film in 1935 in *Mutiny on the Bounty*, and though it's considered a film classic, it's rather a tame affair for current viewers, presented so simplistically in black-and-white terms that it is practically *Billy Budd* without the philosophy. Charles Laughton's performance is not his subtlest; Captain Bligh is a sadistic monster from the very beginning, and even given the mores of the time, one wonders how he ever came to command. Clark Gable as Fletcher Christian is, well, Clark Gable, an all-American hero with no attempt at an English accent, humorously laid back until action is called for. Tahiti as depicted is thirties' all-purpose Polynesia, and much too time is spent on Franchot Tone as what must have been the British navy's oldest midshipman, symbolizing the man of intellect (against Gable's man of action) because he's compiling a Tahitian/English dictionary, and coming off the worse for it (men of intellect were not big heroes in the thirties).

The 1962 version of *Mutiny on the Bounty* gave the story in a good deal more detail, with almost an hour more of length than the earlier version. The attempt to round the Horn, which eventually fails, is exciting and absolutely convincing, and the recreation of a Tahitian culture as yet almost untainted by that of the West is as close to authentic as one could wish (except that bare breasts were still a censorship problem, so the Tahitian women wore a vast amount of leis topside).

Opposite:
Mutiny on the Bounty (1935): The *Bounty*, 1935 version.

Overleaf:
Mutiny on the Bounty (1962): Tahiti as seen in the remake was suitably idyllic but also visually authentic.

This was big-scale moviemaking at its most exuberant, and it was backed by some fascinating performances. Trevor Howard's Captain Bligh is not the larger-than-life monster that Laughton gave us; here is a narrow-minded man with a touch of paranoia determined to win success in his first command, and going about it with methods not particularly unusual for the time. Marlon Brando's surprising Fletcher Christian is an overcivilized aristocrat. Only slowly do we realize that there is a keen intelligence beneath the effete veneer, and that an almost modern sensibility is remarking the barbarities of the Captain's behavior and the beauties of the "savage" Tahitian society. It is an elitist performance much decried by the critics.

A third version was *The Bounty* (1985), perfectly competent and perhaps the most straightforward of the three. Mel Gibson was Christian; Anthony Hopkins, Bligh.

FRANCE—18TH CENTURY A.D.

France in the late eighteenth century was in a bad way. She had beggered herself in helping the American colonies, and her current ruler, Louis XVI, did not reflect the glories of the two that came before (XIV and XV). He was an inept man with a passion for hunting and locksmithing. His queen, Marie Antoinette, was a daughter of the powerful Maria Theresa of Austria. During the first years of their marriage, Louis was impotent, and Antoinette established a reputation for spendthrift giddiness which continued despite a certain reformation brought on by motherhood (a boy and a girl). There was a really unfortunate affair of a fabulously expensive necklace she claimed not to have bought. Several bad winters brought famine to France. The Revolution began with a mob of citizens attacking and leveling the fortress prison called the Bastille in Paris. The king and queen were brought from their country palace, Versailles, to Paris as hostages of the revolutionaries, but still nominally holding their thrones. This uneasy state of affairs actually went on for several years, but the king attempted to escape, and was dethroned and beheaded. The queen and a large number of the aristocracy also lost their heads in a reign of terror.

The power vacuum that was left was fought over by innumerable factions, and was eventually filled by a young military genius who took control as the century turned. Napoleon Bonaparte continued the aspirations of the Revolution so long as it suited him, conquered half of Europe in its name with a superbly trained and motivated army, and eventually crowned himself emperor, placing his numerous brothers and sisters on various thrones of Europe. He then put aside his beloved wife Josephine, and married—with an unfortunate precedent—an Austrian princess! His downfall was contributed to by a badly miscalculated invasion of Russia (ruled by Catherine's grandson, Alexander I). Exiled to Elba, a small island in the Mediterranean, he returned to France, gathered his loyal army to his cause, and suffered ultimate defeat at Waterloo, a village in Belgium, against a combination of the forces of Europe. Louis XVI's brother was placed on the throne of France and Napoleon was exiled to another island, this one well out of the way in the South Atlantic. He remained there until his death.

The glamour of the French court has long fascinated moviemakers. An early talky, for instance, purported to tell all about *Madame Dubarry (sic)* (1934), last mistress to Louis XV. Played with a light touch, it is another example of the whitewashing of a notorious woman of history. Here Du Barry is a strumpet, but one with a heart of gold, and a woman of the people to boot. Marie Antoinette (Anita Louise) is the villain, the snobbish Austrian aristocrat who attempts to high hat her royal father-in-law's mistress (though there is a rather touching scene built around the wedding night of Antoinette and the impotent dauphin). Du Barry as portrayed by the Mexican actress Dolores del Rio is a high-spirited girl playing on the king's lust: when she wants to take a sleigh ride in summer, Paris is denuded of sugar, which is used to coat the grounds of Versailles to satisfy that wish; she invades a state function in her nightgown because she has not yet been formally presented at court. Reginald Owen, who made an art of pomposity, was vastly amusing as Louis XV, a role he had played the year before in *Voltaire*.

If *Le Roi Soleil* had been commissioning movies instead of lavish theatrical spectacles, the result could well have been on the scale of *Marie Antoinette* (1939). There have been more expensive films, certainly, but few have *looked* so rich. The spectacle of Antoinette's arrival at Versailles would have been the high point of any other movie; here it comes early, and later scenes do not suffer by comparison.

In this one it is Antoinette who is really the Good Woman, an innocent princess brought to a lascivious court to marry a doltish dauphin who cannot perform his husbandly duties. (Post-Hollywood censorship code, this was handled obliquely to the point of obscurity.) Her position is ridiculed by the old king's mistress, Du Barry, who sends her a toy cradle as a not-so-subtle gibe. She is used by the king's brother, "Philippe Egalité," the Duc d'Orleans, in a feud with Du Barry, then abandoned by him when it seems she will be returned to Austria. Naturally embittered, Antoinette flings herself into relatively innocent merrymaking, in the process of which she meets a handsome Swedish aristocrat, Count Axel de Fersen, with whom she falls in love. Her passion is returned, but the relationship remains chaste.

The old king dies and Antoinette assumes the responsibility of her position (and motherhood, with the ending of Louis's physical problem), but her reputation remains tarnished. The affair of the diamond necklace is presented as a complex fraud in which the queen is innocent. Comes the revolution—Versailles is invaded by the mob, the royal household is moved to Paris, there is an attempted escape (engineered by the faithful Axel) that fails, the king and queen are imprisoned, he is executed and eventually she, too, rides the tumbrel to the guillotine.

It's all filmed with a lavish use of time and space (the film is long, the sets are enormous), and while sometimes ponderous, it is never boring. Norma Shearer is innocent, brittle, troubled, and tragic as each is called for, and does each smoothly if not with much depth. She is particularly impressive in the final moments, her hair a wild mass turned white from her horrendous experiences. Tyrone Power as Count Fersen is handsome enough to turn any queen's head, but is still in the young and wooden phase of his career, and is something of a stick. The film is stolen on the male side by Robert Morley making his film debut as the pathetic Louis XVI, but he's given some stiff competition by John Barrymore as the old king and Joseph Schildkraut as Philippe Egalité, who changes his eyebrows to suit the current political climate (Jean Harlow—arched for the court, straight and stern for the Republic). The eternal tough lady, Gladys George, deserves mention as Du Barry, as does Anita Louise, who in a curious trick of casting follows her Antoinette in *Madame Dubarry* by playing Antoinette's best friend, the Princess DeLamballe.

Basically, the film's philosophy is a royalist one, not surprising considering its central figure. The message seems to be that the French Revolution was inevitable and that Louis and his queen were powerless pawns of destiny, despite all their good intentions.

Opposite, above:
Mutiny on the Bounty (1962): Fletcher
Christian (Marlon Brando, foreground left) and
Captain Bligh (Trevor Howard, center), 1962
version.

Opposite, below:
The Bounty: Fletcher Christian (Mel Gibson,
left) and Captain Bligh (Anthony Hopkins),
1985 version.

Mutiny on the Bounty (1962): The *Bounty*, 1962
version.

The Bounty: The *Bounty*, 1985 version.

Madame Dubarry: Not having been presented at court, Madame Dubarry (Dolores Del Rio) decides to attend a state function in her nightgown.

Marie Antoinette: A very different DuBarry (Gladys George) has a *tête-à-tête* with Louis XV (John Barrymore).

Marie Antoinette: Norma Shearer, in the title role, gave new meaning to the term "clothes horse," considering the weight of the costumes.

Opposite:
Marie Antoinette: There is some doubt that Versailles in the 1780s could ever have matched Hollywood in the 1930s.

Orphans of the Storm: Lillian and Dorothy Gish were the orphans; the storm was the French revolution.

Opposite, above:
Orphans of the Storm: Henriette (Lillian Gish, on balcony) hears her lost foster sister, the blind Louise (Dorothy Gish), singing in the street.

Opposite, below:
Orphans of the Storm: Henriette pleads with the Revolutionary Assembly to spare her life and that of her aristocratic lover.

D. W. Griffith's *Orphans of the Storm* (1922) gives quite another view of the French Revolution. Lovely young Henriette takes her foster sister Louise to Paris in hopes of finding a cure for her blindness. Barely are they off the coach when Henriette is kidnapped by a marquis whose lust she has aroused, and Louise, left helpless, is made off with by a brutal beggar woman and forced into a life of—horrors!—street singing. After harrowing months of near misses, close encounters, brushes with death, brushes with fates worse than death, and then on top of everything else, the Revolution, they are brought together as Henriette is sentenced to the guillotine for sheltering an aristocrat, the young Chevalier de Vaudray, with whom she has fallen in love. He also is to die. This heartless sentence leads to a showdown between Robespierre and Danton, whose life Henriette has saved in one of the rare moments she hasn't been looking for Louise. Danton wins and after a breathtaking gallop to the place of execution, the two lovers are pardoned and reunited, as are the two sisters. As it happens, Louise is the long-lost daughter of the Chevalier's mother; her sight is restored and everyone lives happily ever after.

Griffith alternates his melodrama of the two orphans with huge crowd scenes and vistas of revolutionary Paris. The revolution as shown consists mostly of the attack on the Bastille (spectacularly reenacted) and most of the population of Paris dancing the carmagnole lasciviously in the streets. One would think from the script that it all (from the fall of the Bastille to the Reign of Terror) took place in a couple of weeks.

The frequent explanatory titles give Griffith's highly idiosyncratic view of the conflict: Danton is "the Abraham Lincoln of France"; Robespierre is "the original pussyfooter," and it is his leadership that leads the nation to ANARCHY AND BOLSHEVISM, which in a later title we are warned to avoid at all costs.

It is somehow ironic that the Gish sisters play Henriette and Louise, foster sisters in the script. Lillian's wistful quality has been long celebrated, but surprisingly Dorothy as the blind Louise sometimes has the stronger presence and the greater beauty. Henriette's beloved Chevalier de Vaudray is the very young, handsome Joseph Schildkraut who would go on to play another French aristocrat, the mincing Duc D'Orleans, in *Marie Antoniette* as well as many another great character role.

These movies were an American view of the French Revolution—or, more correctly, of the legends of the French Revolution. A French view was given by *La Marseillaise* (1938), and the perspective is startlingly different. The disparity is not simply that of nationalistic philosophy; the approach was also highly original by the Hollywood standards of the time. Writer-director Jean Renoir gives us the Revolution's beginnings, not from Paris but from the provinces, and not from the top, but from the bottom. He tells the story of a group of ordinary citizens of Marseilles—a peasant, a tradesman, an accountant, and so forth—who are caught up in the Revolution and who become part of the provincial army that marches on Paris, taking with them a "Prussian marching song" to which French words have been set. It is, of course, "The Marseillaise," and the film is in a way its story—the human characters are almost incidental. They take part in the battle of the Tuileries, which was responsible for the final fall of the monarchy; it is a stunning scene, certainly one of the most realistic battles—in its confusion and terror—ever filmed. The glimpses we get of Louis and Marie Antoinette are also refreshingly different—here is a shrewd, educated couple determined to keep their position at all costs, not the romantic queen and cartoon king represented elsewhere. The movie ends with our band of Marseillaises, much reduced, on the way to the battle of Valmy in 1792, in which Prussian and Austrian antirevolutionary forces were stopped

Orphans of the Storm: D. W. Griffith's re-creation of the Place de la Revolution.

La Marseillaise: The aftermath of the rivetingly
re-created battle of the Tuileries.

from invading France. "The Marseillaise" is now the anthem of the
Revolution.

Napoleon Bonaparte has been almost as omnipresent on the screen as he
was on the stage of history, but only one major movie has been devoted to his
life, and that only to the early years—Abel Gance's silent *Napoleon* (1927).
This lengthy and ambitious project takes Napoleon only through the Italian
campaign, which was to all intents and purposes the beginning of his meteoric
career.

Gance took as a philosophical guideline the words of St. Beauve—"Reveal
the truth of the whole through the non-truth of the details" (which can apply to
most forms of historical drama from Shakespeare to *Lawrence of Arabia*). He
was technically innovative and esthetically ambitious, qualities reflected in
Napoleon. Its initial version was well over three hours in length and at times
needed three projectors for a primitive version of a wide screen (called
"Polyvision"). The problems raised led him to make a number of other versions, shorter and re-edited (one in stereophonic sound).

The movie opens with Napoleon leading a snowball fight at the military
academy at Briennes in 1781 and careers through various incidents in his
early life: an initial encounter with Josephine de Beauharnais in a Paris street;
an escape from Corsica alone in a small boat fighting a sirocco and using a
French flag for a sail; his formal meeting with Josephine at a "victims' ball"
during the Terror (admittance only if one has been imprisoned or a close relative has been executed); and the recapture of the besieged port of Toulon.

These are intercut with scenes of the progress of the Revolution and Napoleon's gradual rise to political and military power, culminating in the Italian campaign, the battle of Montenotte, and the emergence of "La Grande Armée" from a ragtag mob to the great force behind Napoleon's will. These final scenes are in the three-screen process, and Gance uses them not only for panoramic effect, but often with three different images attempting a sort of visual polyphony.

Napoleon is something of a problem for a modern audience, even in the superbly reconstructed version released in 1981. There are the inevitable silent-screen conventions in acting and script, which is rife with omens from Napoleon's childhood pet, an eagle, to a palmist telling Josephine just after her first encounter with Napoleon that she would be queen. Much of the innovative editing and visual manipulation seems self-conscious and arty to eyes more accustomed to the seamlessness of modern cinema. And given the number of versions of the film, there is no final form to judge. It's as if Shakespeare had left us a dozen Hamlets, long, short, edited, re-edited, and rearranged.

A radically different look at Napoleon's life, albeit one at second hand, is given by *Désirée* (1954). Désirée ("desired") indeed; she is a provincial shopkeeper's daughter who meets and loves Napoleon when he is a junior officer posted in the French boondocks. Her sister marries Napoleon's brother Joseph, but the family draws the line at Napoleon—he doesn't have much future, and besides, "one Bonaparte in the family is enough." Nevertheless, her destiny is tied to Napoleon's and through thick, thin, and Josephine, their

Above:
Napoleon: Albert Dieudonné as Napoleon.

Top:
Napoleon: La grande armée in the making in Abel Gance's epic film of Napoleon's rise.

Désirée: The set and costumes for this scene in which Napoleon (Marlon Brando) crowns Josephine (Merle Oberon) bear a studied (to say the least) resemblance to the historical painting by David.

paths entwine, though she eventually marries one of Napoleon's most trusted generals, Count Bernadotte. When the count is elected by the Swedes to become their crown prince, *voilà!*—Désirée is Queen of Sweden.

She returns to France just in time for Napoleon's downfall, and on the terrace of Malmaison, Josephine's home, persuades him to surrender rather than kill himself. At least *Désirée* doesn't have her stowing away on the ship to St. Helena.

This curious variation on history would be of the utmost inanity if it weren't for the leading players, Marlon Brando and Jean Simmons, who somehow contrive to play it like a drawing-room comedy, and between them give the picture a charming playfulness. Brando is a marvelous Napoleon, the only one in film with the streak of humor that so many historical anecdotes record. Simmons, who seems to be able to salvage any role she attempts, makes Désirée undeniably desirable, and charming as well. Even the gorgeous but usually humorless Merle Oberon seems infected, and her Josephine shares the general good humor while regarding Désirée throughout the film with justifiable suspicion. Everyone looks splendid in Napoleonic uniforms and Empire gowns, and there is a knockout re-creation of Napoleon's coronation, reproducing the painting by Jean-Louis David. The final encounter between the two principals achieves an almost surrealist grandeur—the terrace at Malmaison (in reality a comparatively modest estate) sports acres of white marble, set against a sky of searing Maxfield Parrish blue. *Désirée* is hardly history, but it's a lot of fun.

The Pride and the Passion: Cary Grant, as a British officer, looks dubiously at the cannon he is to ordered to transport across Spain in the Peninsular Wars.

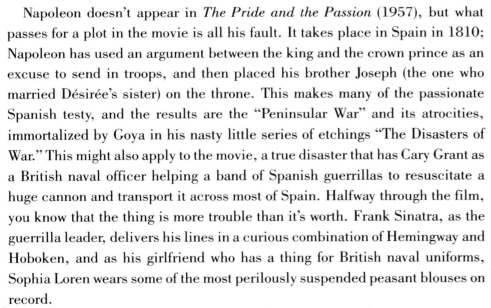

The Pride and the Passion: The cannon is hidden by the guerrillas in a Spanish cathedral.

Napoleon doesn't appear in *The Pride and the Passion* (1957), but what passes for a plot in the movie is all his fault. It takes place in Spain in 1810; Napoleon has used an argument between the king and the crown prince as an excuse to send in troops, and then placed his brother Joseph (the one who married Désirée's sister) on the throne. This makes many of the passionate Spanish testy, and the results are the "Peninsular War" and its atrocities, immortalized by Goya in his nasty little series of etchings "The Disasters of War." This might also apply to the movie, a true disaster that has Cary Grant as a British naval officer helping a band of Spanish guerrillas to resuscitate a huge cannon and transport it across most of Spain. Halfway through the film, you know that the thing is more trouble than it's worth. Frank Sinatra, as the guerrilla leader, delivers his lines in a curious combination of Hemingway and Hoboken, and as his girlfriend who has a thing for British naval uniforms, Sophia Loren wears some of the most perilously suspended peasant blouses on record.

In the immortal words of Radar O'Reilly when first encountering Tolstoy: "War *and* Peace?" Napoleon makes several cameo appearances in the work, and in the two big films that were made from it. The first (1956) might be called the NATO version—the leading actors were American, British, Belgian, and Italian as well as Austrian, Czech, and Swedish, and the resulting mélange of accents prompted much of the criticism leveled at it. It was, nevertheless, a big, beautiful movie, impeccably produced.

Audrey Hepburn was born to play Natasha Rostova, the young aristocrat

Overleaf, left:
War and Peace (1956): This is peace—the ball at which Natasha meets Andrei (Audrey Hepburn and Mel Ferrer, foreground).

Overleaf, above right:
War and Peace (1956): And this is war—as the Russian troops march through Moscow.

Overleaf, below right:
War and Peace (1956): And this is defeat—as Napoleon's army struggles through the vastness of Russia in winter.

whose transition from child to woman lies at the heart of the sprawling novel. This is not Scarlett or Amber; here is an intelligent, civilized girl who makes one tragic adolescent mistake. A year of waiting before marriage is required by the eccentric father of the man she loves, Prince Andrey Bolkonski; in that year, which she resents bitterly, her heart is stolen by a ne'er-do-well and there is an aborted attempt to elope. The too-upright Andrey cannot forgive her, and they are reunited only after he received a mortal wound during Napoleon's invasion of Russia, the broad canvas against which the personal drama is played.

As counterpoint to Natasha's emotional development, there is the intellectual—or more correctly, philosophical—development of her father's young friend, Pierre, an immature bear of a man who does not join in the fighting, but observes the battle of Borodino, which, lost by the Russians, determined the fate of Mosow—to be evacuated and burned as Napoleon enters. Pierre stays in the city, and, as a prisoner, takes part in the horrendous French winter retreat. He survives, as does Natasha; the odd pair, the swan and the bear, are united at the end.

Pierre is presented in the unlikely person of Henry Fonda, who can bumble with the best but is hardly bearlike. He is, however, convincing if you can forget Tolstoy's description. There is a host of minor characters; even though many of the novel's subplots are abandoned, the cast is a large one. Mel Ferrer is Andrey, aristocratic, too sensitive, and as questioning in his own dutybound way as Pierre. The striking Anita Ekberg is Pierre's first wife, the beautiful but vicious Helene, who thinks it a joke to encourage Natasha's flirtation with the worthless Dholokov. Herbert Lom is an impressive Napoleon, first seen at the battle of Austerlitz and again in Moscow. Oscar Homolka has a character actor's field day as Napoleon's one-eyed nemesis, General Kutuzov, as does Sir John Mills in a very different mode, in a brief role as a fellow prisoner of Pierre's.

There are many remarkable scenes. Natasha's first ball is Imperial Russia at its height (and Hepburn at her most heartbreakingly beautiful). The evacuation of Moscow and its subsequent burning can rival that of Atlanta. The trek through the snowbound wastes of Russia in the retreat, with its endless lines of men on a route strewn with corpses, is harrowingly staged. And the battle scenes—Borodino in particular—are memorable for the vast forces brought into play for the camera and the reality of the result.

Memorable, that is, until the Russian *War and Peace* was released. This staggering achievement was originally conceived as four separate films. It took four years to produce (1963–67) at a cost that has been estimated at up to a hundred million dollars (and proved that totalitarian governments could make bigger movies as well as the trains run on time). The results are hard to judge, since it was released in the United States in a two-part truncated version (which only ran about seven hours), and was execrably dubbed.

But so far as one could tell through uneven cutting and stilted English dialogue, all of Tolstoy was there, gorgeously costumed and set. The battle scenes—again Borodino in particular—were of unparalleled scope, especially several scenes shot from the air, in which the whole battlefield seems to appear on the screen, punctuated with the squares of Russian infantry surrounded by the circles of wheeling French cavalry, all overlaid with clouds of cannon smoke.

The conventions of Russian acting and makeup, as well as the atrocious dubbing and sheer numbers of the cast, make it difficult to speak of the actors with any authority. But it can be noted that the West had an edge in Audrey Hepburn (of which there is probably only one per century) though the Soviet

Opposite, above:
War and Peace (1963–67): A Russian Napoleon; the actor is Vladislav Strzhelchik.

Opposite, below:
War and Peace (1963–67): The battle scenes were the glory of the gigantic Russian-made version of the Tolstoy novel.

Waterloo: This re-creation of Napoleon's final
battle owed much to director Sergei
Bondarchuk's *War and Peace*.

Waterloo: An American Napoleon; the actor is
Rod Steiger.

Natasha, the young dancer Ludmila Savelyeva (who practically grew up with the production) was *almost* as radiant. (The director cheated a bit by surrounding her entrance with a scintillation of sparkling lights, which Hepburn seemed to evoke without special effects.) And that said director, Sergei Bondarchuk, was not only responsible for this whole vast enterprise, but played the second central character, Pierre, very capably, and was physically an absolute ringer for Tolstoy's description.

This production had a curious footnote in *Waterloo* (1970), a combined East-West production directed by Bondarchuk and starring Rod Steiger as Napoleon and Christopher Plummer as the Duke of Wellington. It was more or less a collage of the events leading up to Napoleon's last battle, ending with a re-creation of the battle itself. Not as clear as it might have been, it repeated many of the effects of Borodino in *War and Peace*, and again the battle scenes are spectacular. It concludes with a lengthy panoramic shot of the devastated battlefield after Napoleon's defeat that might well be the last word in the horrors-of-war school of cinema.

THE MODERN AGE— CENTURIES 19 AND 20

THE UNITED STATES—19th CENTURY A.D.

The cinema is a twentieth-century art, but there are almost as many movies set in the nineteenth century as in the twentieth. Temporal propinquity was augmented by the fact that the United States was the dominant force in moviemaking, and most of its history was confined to the nineteenth century. (It's an obvious but unremarked fact that most Westerns are historical films.) There are subtler factors at work also—the "historical" movie becomes something else when laid in post-Napoleonic times. For one thing, much of the last century was within the memory of the earlier filmmakers and audiences. There were people still alive when Gone With the Wind *was made who remembered the Civil War, and for a large part of the population,* The Birth of a Nation *was a docudrama, a reconstruction (as it were) of something they had lived through. Early movie Westerns were often made by people who remembered "the Wild West"—real covered wagons and ten-gallon hats were available as props and the two locomotives that met at the completion of the transcontinental railroad played themselves in* The Iron Horse—*and their startling authenticity shines through the artificial melodrama of their plots. For another, still photography had recorded much of the nineteenth century with accuracy. The look of places, fashions, and particularly people were known factors, not guesswork based on paintings, dressings, and/or archaeological findings.*

So most movies laid in the last century are essentially dramas, comedies, or thrillers with bowlers and bustles. But material for spectacle was found there also. Most such movies, as noted above, were concerned with the history of the United States; they had either to do with the two wars that were fought in the United States itself (that of 1812 and the tragic Civil War) or with the epic potential of the opening of the West.

During the War of 1812, the last of the pirates, Jean Lafitte, whose operations centered around the port of New Orleans (newly acquired by the United States from France), threw in his lot with the American forces and helped Andrew Jackson fight off the British.

55 Days At Peking: The Great Gate of Peking was the movie's *big* set.

The Buccaneer (1958): The great days of
Caribbean piracy were over by the nineteenth
century, but Jean Lafitte & Co. carried on the
tradition lustily, judging by this sack of the
good ship *Corinthian*.

The Buccaneer (1938): Jean Lafitte (Fredric
March) tangles with a member of the New
Orleans aristocracy (Ian Keith).

The Alamo: The Alamo, its siege and fall, were re-created in a big way in this 1960 movie.

Lafitte's actions were probably less due to any devotion to the principals of his new government than awareness that the British were more to be feared than the Americans, but it made for a romantic legend of which Cecil B. DeMille took full advantage in *The Buccaneer* (1938). It featured a curly-haired, mustachioed Fredric March as a sensitive Lafitte, supposedly in love with a high-born New Orleans Creole, and an engaging Hungarian actress, Franciska Gaal, as a Dutch serving girl who wins his affections and sails off into the sunset with him after some spectacular battles on land and sea. Gaal, whose American career was interrupted by World War II, provided the DeMille light touch of the thirties with a classic soubrette performance. And Lafitte indeed did disappear after the war—his end is one of history's minor mysteries.

A remake of *The Buccaneer* appeared twenty years later (1958), produced by DeMille but directed by Anthony Quinn, who had had a secondary role in the first version. DeMille might as well have directed; the film had all the earmarks of his postwar work, particularly in the lack of humor (the Dutch girl was dropped entirely) and a corresponding heaviness. Despite the star qualities of Yul Brynner, who made a dashing Lafitte, Charlton Heston as Andrew Jackson, and the beautiful Claire Bloom as the aristocratic love interest, it was a leaden and lackluster movie.

The siege of the Alamo technically didn't take place on United States soil, since it occurred in Texas's struggle to free itself from Mexico, but with the entry of Texas into the Union the incident entered American mythology. It was put on the screen in *The Alamo* (1960), and the final shootout has as much blood and thunder as any Texan could wish. But getting there is a chore what with John Wayne being as folksy as all get out as Davy Crockett, making peace between Richard Widmark as a sullen Jim Bowie and Laurence Harvey as the by-the-book Colonel William Travis.

There is a terrible irony in the fact that *The Birth of a Nation* (1915) perhaps contributed more than any other single film to the creation of the conventions of the art of the cinema, while dealing with a period that still arouses the most heated of feelings in the United States, and dealing with it in a manner that has become more rather than less controversial and distasteful to many over the years. Director D. W. Griffith chose to portray the Civil War though Thomas Dixon's novel *The Clansman* (as the movie was also called initally), which showed the conflict primarily from the Southern point of view (though portraying Abraham Lincoln as a heroic character) and, even more controversially, extended into the bitter Reconstruction period when the North, without Lincoln's humanitarian guidance, took its revenge on the South.

The melodramatic plot revolves around the many romantic entanglements of the children of a prominent Southern family, the Camerons, and a family of the North, the Stonemans. Sons of both families are killed or wounded in the war (re-created in epic battle scenes); Ben, the eldest Cameron son, is captured and saved from death on a false charge by Lincoln himself. After the war, Ben is instrumental in the formation of the Ku Klux Klan, which is presented as a necessary force to counter Northern repression. The final episode is the Klan's spectacular ride to save Elsie Stoneman from the clutches of the nefarious half-breed, Silas Lynch, who had earlier been responsible for the death of Ben's sister.

Birth of a Nation, as well as being a major milestone in film technique, showed the power of the film as a social force, not only portraying history but making it. Highly controversial even in its time, it is held responsible by many for the pre–World War I revival of the Klan in its most unpleasant aspects. At this remove, it should be regarded as a product of an era that still remembered the period it portrayed, with concomitant truths and biases.

Gone With the Wind: The scene that left not a dry eye, Yankee *or* Southern, in the house— the thousands of Confederate troops dying in the sun.

Gone With the Wind: Scarlett (Vivien Leigh), in that memorable calico dress that got more bedraggled by the moment, can't believe that Dr. Meade (Harry Davenport), who knows something about birthin' babies, won't help.

Perhaps it was the very controversy that was raised by *The Birth of a Nation* that caused the Civil War to lose popularity as a subject for the cinema. Whatever the reasons, by the mid 1930s it was regarded as box-office poison. But then. . . .

Fiddle-dee-dee! What can be said about *Gone With the Wind* (1939)? It may not be the greatest movie ever made, but it *is* the finest example of Hollywood moviemaking as a craft. Here was a riveting story with a selfishly wicked heroine, superbly acted and beautifully set against an epically reproduced period of war and turmoil. In historical terms, it was an interesting contrast to *The Birth of a Nation.* Covering the same period—the Civil War and Reconstruction—it had no battle scenes and more or less concentrated on the home front, but since the home front encompassed the evacuation and burning of Atlanta, there was no shortage of excitement. Both the heroine and the hero were social misfits, though Scarlett, in her way, was the epitome of the spoiled progeny of a slave-owning aristocracy (the loving Melanie represents the other side of Southern womanhood). It even gingerly explored the sort of Southern vigilantism that resulted in the Klan, though without being nearly as explicit as the earlier film.

The screen tests for Scarlett by the female stars of the period have been made public, and they are all unthinkable after having seen Vivien Leigh. The same holds true for the part of Rhett—no one but Clark Gable can be envisioned in the role. Casting and performances were faultless (and proved the kinship of the Southern aristocracy with their British cousins in that three of

Duel in the Sun: Like mother, like daughter: the half-breed Pearl (Jennifer Jones) dances outside the gambling palace where her mother performs.

the four leading actors were British born) with a couple of minor quibbles—Leslie Howard was not physically the young Southern Adonis that Ashley should have been, and the ringleted pudding purported to be the child of Scarlett and Rhett was an unfortunate choice.

There is some sort of irony in the written prologue to the film—"Look for it only in books, for it is no more than a dream remembered," it says of the culture of the Old South; the same can now be said of the Hollywood that made *GWTW*. Never again will we see its like or the like of what it produced—that kind of moviemaking is also gone with the wind.

Producer David O. Selznick hoped to reproduce the success of *Gone With the Wind* with his postwar production of *Duel in the Sun* (1946). This didn't happen for various reasons: the plot and its milieu were steamily Western (Texas) rather than romantically Southern; the stars didn't have the magic of the *GWTW* team; and the background—the invasion by the railroads of the great Texas cattle ranches that had developed after the Civil War—while reflecting the epic quality of the push westward, didn't have the universality of the North–South conflict.

It *did* share with the earlier film the quality of echt moviemaking. The plot was melodrama pushed to the limit, with a visually lush production taking full advantage of the splendors of the Southwest as complement. The heroine (?) is Pearl Chavez, the half-breed daughter of a highborn Southerner now living by his skill at gambling and an Indian woman of questionable reputation. The father kills the mother and her lover, and, sentenced to death, sends Pearl to his cousin Laura Belle, a fading daughter of the Old South married to a Texas cattle baron, Jason McCanles, whose holdings seem to consist of half the state.

The barely civilized Pearl desires to emulate Laura Belle's ladylike ways, but the two McCanles sons raise problems. She is attracted to the older Jesse, a serious, progressive young man; when he rejects her she submits to Lewt, the spoiled, hell-raising younger one, who shares his father's violent prejudice against Indians. Pearl finally agrees to marry Sam, the mild-mannered straw boss of the ranch; Lewt, regarding Pearl as his property, kills Sam and becomes an outlaw, secretly supported by his father whom he repays by blowing up trains.

The personal drama is played out against the coming of the railroads; there had been a confrontation between the vast forces of the ranch—a veritable army of cowboys—and the railroad crew when the line reached the border of Spanish Bit, the McCanles ranch. When the cavalry arrived, Jason refused to fire on the United States flag and the railroad went through. The older son, Jesse, has joined forces with the railroad interests; when he returns to the area, Lewt shoots him in a classic cow town confrontation and flees into the desert. Pearl, still sustaining her love for Jesse, finds out where he is hiding and follows him. In the resulting duel, carried out against the barren red-rock hills of the Texas outback, both are fatally shot, and they die in each other's arms.

This overwrought scenario teetered precariously on the edge of silliness and, according to many critics, often fell in. But the sheer splendor of the production carried it; here were all the clichés of the Western movie, brought to an ultimate extreme. Three sequences transcend the script. The first is the opener, in the Presidio, the dance hall in which Pearl's mother dances. This is indeed a gambling palace; it's about as large as the Baths of Caracella. With its endless bar, innumerable whirling gambling wheels, and an atmosphere you could cut with a machete, the influence of Josef von Sternberg (*The Scarlet Empress*), who is rumored to have had an uncredited hand in the direction, seems clear. Pearl's mother is played (or more correctly, danced) by the exotic Tilly Losch. Cheered on by the enormous, lustful crowd, she eventually mounts the bar and circles it, wiggling erotically and firing off pistols. It's a bangup opener; the senses are already overloaded.

Centrally located in the film is the gathering of the forces from the far-flung reaches of Spanish Bit. As the major alarm bell of the ranch is rung, more and more bells pick it up across the vast distances of the spread, and there is a long, speedily cut sequence of groups of cowboys coming from every direction and merging into a tidal wave of men and horses.

The finale, beginning with Pearl's trek across the desert in search of Lewt, is a masterpiece of cinematic construction, dominated by intercut shots of the blazing sun. Helped by every element, from the costuming (Jennifer Jones, as Pearl, is dressed in a wonderfully sleazy cotton skirt and blouse that shows every perspiration stain) to the gradually intensifying score, the scene builds to a feverish pitch, concluding with the fatally wounded Pearl crawling through the rocks and dust to reach the dying Lewt's side. One's fingertips and ribs ache in sympathy with each painful advance and jarring fall.

Jennifer Jones had a field day breaking her good girl image (*The Song of Bernadette*) with the role of Pearl. The character, despite the ambiguity of

Duel in the Sun: In this larger-than-life Western, even the saloons are epic. Tilly Losch, as the heroine's Indian mother, wows the crowd at the Presidio.

Opposite:
Duel in the Sun: Jennifer Jones, breaking her "Bernadette" image as Pearl Chavez, managed to summon up a good imitation of sleaze (with help from the costumer).

The Iron Horse: The locomotives in this version of the event are the actual ones that met at Ogden, Utah, when the two parts of the transcontinental railroad came together.

Opposite, above:

Union Pacific: The DeMille concept of the two parts of the transcontinental railroad finally coming together with the driving of the golden spike.

Opposite, below:

Union Pacific: Indians hunt down and kill the iron horse that is invading their territory.

"well-meaning girl gone wrong," is hardly a subtle one, and Jones played it as unsubtly as possible, with great success. The young Gregory Peck was also playing against type as the devilish Lewt. The struggle was sometimes too evident; some of the Western dialogue just didn't work in that glorious baritone voice. Joseph Cotten was, well, Joseph Cotten, as Jesse.

The secondary characters were as juicy as the leading roles: a vast amount of scenery was well chewed by Lionel Barrymore as the older McCanles, and Lillian Gish, as Laura Belle, held her own as the last of the antebellum ladies with the force of a freight car full of lavender. Butterfly McQueen walked off with every one of her scenes just as she had in *Gone With the Wind* and in much the same role. Walter Huston as the "Sin Killer," a Bible-thumping itinerant preacher, played so broadly (and effectively) as to inspire a printed on-screen disclaimer during the early runs. And Tilly Losch, as noted above, brings down the house in her brief, almost wordless appearance as Pearl's mother.

Duel in the Sun did not do for the West what *Gone With the Wind* did for the South. Nevertheless, it took the western, as a reflection of a particular time and place in American history, and made from it a vividly spectacular epic.

The dramatic westward movement of the railroads provided fodder for many another film. An early one was *The Iron Horse* (1924), the first part of which is mostly devoted to vignettes of the Union Pacific line building westward from Omaha to join the Central Pacific building eastward from Sacramento. Out of these emerges a plot concerning a young pony express rider (George O'Brien), the daughter of the major contractor on the Union Pacific (Madge Bellamy), and a lot of skulduggery to do with land rights and finding a shortcut through the mountains. Due to a lovers' misunderstanding, he departs to work for the Central Pacific, conveniently providing an excuse for the lovers to be reunited when the two lines meet at Ogden, Utah.

Periodic action is supplied by a series of Indian attacks on trains and construction sites. (At one point a band of Indians gallops by the workers, firing wildly; the laborers calmly exchange picks for guns, fire back, and then resume working. One almost expects the remark, "They were late today.")

Comic relief is provided by the antagonism between the Irish and Italian workers, the rough and ready justice of the ever-moving "end of track" head-

212

Northwest Mounted Police: The native
Americans provided most of the spectacle in
this drama of the Riel Revolution in Canada.
Here a troop of "Mounties" gingerly enters an
encampment.

quarters, and such characters as "Ruby," noted in a title as "the bright—but
not too particular—star of the Arabian Nights dance tent." Cameo appearances are made by Buffalo Bill (who received his name from supplying buffalo
meat to the workers), Wild Bill Hickok, and Ulysses S. Grant. Director John
Ford here is already using those sweeping panoramic shots of the western
landscape—particularly of a cattle drive coming north from Texas with beef
for the workers—with which he would become associated. And again, there is
a startling feel of authenticity; the events depicted had occurred within the
memory of many still alive when *The Iron Horse* was made, and the locomotives
used in the final sequence were the two originals that had met at Ogden.

   Much of the same ground is covered in Cecil B. DeMille's *Union Pacific*. It
opens in 1865, with Lincoln signing the bill that would send the railroads west.
The major part of the action occurs in 1868, on the Union Pacific stretch
between Cheyenne and Ogden (the action of *The Iron Horse* is primarily between North Platte and Cheyenne); much of the film's ongoing tension is based
on the need to build the track quickly. Molly Monahan, an immigrant Irish girl
who acts as postmistress for the line, meets Jeff Butler, a young troubleshooter

for the railroad company. Their courtship is erratic, since she must usually be at the "end of track," where the building is, and he must be constantly traveling, especially since there is trouble afoot from rival railroads and political influences.

In the ten months it takes to get to Ogden, there are train wrecks, Indian attacks on trains, relief trains charging across burning trestle bridges, and trains sliding down snow-covered mountainsides. In short, the trains are the heroes of the movie (and pretty spectacular they are), though ever-tough Barbara Stanwyck shows up through the steam to good effect as Molly, and Joel McCrea is a charmingly laid-back, though of course two-fisted, love interest. Here again, the lovers come together at Ogden as the two lines do, and no, we won't dwell on the possible symbolism of the golden spike.

CANADA—19TH CENTURY A.D.

The Riel Rebellion was in a sense Canada's French and Indian War, since it was a rebellion against the government by Indians and French/Indian mixed bloods, the Métis, who established their own nation. Much of the fighting on the government's side was done by the Northwest Mounted Police, which would become the Royal Canadian Mounted Police.

Cecil B. DeMille chose the Riel Rebellion as the setting for *Northwest Mounted Police* (1940). To make the movie more acceptable to American filmgoers, the script brought into the proceedings a Texas Ranger (with the unfortunate name of Dusty Rivers) who is on the trail of a rebellion leader who had committed murder in Texas.

Rivers unofficially joins the Mounties, becomes involved in the war, and falls in love with a district nurse whose fiancé is a Mountie officer. Her brother, also a Mountie, is entangled with a wild half-breed woman (daughter of the fugitive Rivers is seeking) and neglects his duty because of her, but redeems himself heroically and, of course, fatally. In the end, Rivers gets his man, in true Mountie tradition.

There are ambushes, Indians, and battles aplenty, but DeMille wisely left the spectacle to the breathtaking Canadian scenery. Gary Cooper was another

laid-back, two fisted hero of the type DeMille semed to favor in this period. Using his underrated comedic talents, Cooper also supplied some needed lighter moments in his interplay with the spit and polish Mounties, and in one wonderful short scene when he accidentally uncovers an anatomy chart in the nurse's office. His split second of flustered reaction as he hastily covers it up again is sheer comic inspiration.

The icy Madeleine Carroll actually managed some warmth in the standard good girl role of the nurse. She had stiff competition from Paulette Goddard as the bad girl, Louvette, who delivered her lines in a peculiar form of French-Canadian baby talk and wound herself around any male in the vicinity.

MEXICO—19TH CENTURY A.D.

On the other side of the United States, Mexico, too, was having turbulent times in the nineteenth century. One of the more dramatic periods occurred when France under the Second Empire sent in an army of occupation and its own choice of ruler (an Austrian Archduke) for Mexico, to be opposed by liberal Mexican forces led by a singularly undashing figure, a full-blooded Indian named Benito Juárez.

Hollywood chose to chronicle this event in one of the many biopics tailored for the multifaceted character actor Paul Muni, in the title role of *Juarez* (1939). The opposition was led by Brian Aherne with the longest, curliest side-whiskers ever seen in Hollywood, as the "Emperor" (courtesy of France) Maximilian. Bette Davis was his unfortunate empress, Carlotta.

The two were presented as a pair of royal European do-gooders, totally unaware that the *ancien régime* had ended in Europe and never even begun in America, led into the folly of attempting to rule Mexico as pawns of Napoleon III (Claude Rains), a view with which history generally agrees. The tragedy plays itself out as, despite attempts by the well-meaning royals to come to terms with the equally well-meaning Juárez, the inevitable forces of greed and power hunger drive them apart. Maximilian is captured and shot, and Carlotta, returned to France to seek aid from the nefarious French emperor, goes mad.

Despite a stellar cast, a sumptuous production, and a valiant attempt to clarify the various force at work in the never-simple politics of Mexico, the movie simply didn't jell and turned out to be a lengthy bore. It's almost worth seeing, however, for Rains's turn as Napoleon, and for the formidable Gale Sondergaard as his empress, Eugénie (who, of course, wears some formidable hats). An interesting piece of casting, also, was that of John Garfield as the young General Díaz, who (after the movie ends) would seize power and rule Mexico for many years.

SOUTH AFRICA—19TH CENTURY A.D.

The big theater of the nineteenth century was the British Empire, and it was a theater with an endless variety of sets and costumes. Its trials and tribulations and those of its soldiers, real and fictional, have made up the stuff of a thousand films.

For sheer excitement none of them can beat Zulu (1964). It recreates an 1879 incident in which a small band of British soldiers held their own against a Zulu army at a place called Rorke's Drift in South Africa. What could have been an ordinary stiff-upper-lip siege exercise became an enthralling and spectacular suspense movie by dint of sensational photography, a tight script, and brilliant

Juarez: The court of Mexico, ruled very briefly by the French puppets, Emperor Maximilian (Brian Aherne) and Empress Carlotta (Bette Davis).

Juarez: The people of Mexico are led by Juarez (Paul Muni, center).

Zulu: A rousing moment in a rousing film, as the Zulu army attacks the British.

editing. Most of the last half of the film is concerned with the final battle between the two forces; the Zulus are shown, not as a simple horde of easily mowed-down savages, but as the proud, disciplined warriors that they were, which keeps the outcome all the more in doubt. The spectacle is supplied by the phenomenal South African landscape and the masses of brilliantly bedecked tribesmen. Stanley Baker and Michael Caine also transcend stereotype as officers in charge of the Brits. There is something of a surprise ending—a final gesture on the part of the Zulus that shatters an easy judgment as to which side really emerged triumphant.

SICILY—19TH CENTURY A.D.

The major social drama of the nineteenth century in Europe was the fall of the ancien régime, *the old order of aristocrat and peasant, to a middle class of merchant and manufacturer, which more or less began with a bang with the French Revolution but continued, sometimes peacefully, sometimes with great slaughter, across the continent.*

Almost all American films that had to do with this were rather simplistically on the side of "the people"; the United States, given its relative youth and democratic sympathies, had little insight into the sometimes tragic side of the inevitable defeat of a lifestyle that had existed for many centuries.

Luchino Visconti's *The Leopard* (1963) took this downfall as its thesis. The film was set in the Sicily of 1860 (then the Kingdom of the Two Sicilies). The central figure is an aging Sicilian aristocrat, the Prince of Salina, who attempts to hold on to the old way of life as the storm of civil war bursts around him (this is the period when Garibaldi was attempting to unite all of Italy into one nation). As the three-hour film unfolds, the prince is forced to accept the changes in society, most notably in the fact that his dashing nephew must be allowed to marry beneath him.

It's a lavish production, but more importantly it's an extraordinarily realistic one; there is the feeling that this is how mid-nineteenth-century Sicily really

218

The Leopard: The climax of the film is a remarkably realistic nineteenth-century grand ball, led off by Prince Don Fabrizio Salina (Burt Lancaster), the Leopard himself, and his nephew's bride, Angelica (Claudia Cardinale).

The Leopard: A truly international cast included Alain Delon (left), Cardinale, and Lancaster.

looked. The two most impressive sequences are a trip across the arid Sicilian landscape by coach, in which the passengers are gradually encased in layers of dust and arrive looking like pottery figures, and a grand ball that takes most of the last hour of the film. This is no glamorized version of perfectly hoopskirted ladies and exquisitely groomed men dancing in pristine comfort. The prince's acceptance of the rich bourgeoisie and arrogant military men now a part of his social sphere is emphasized by the *verismo* of the milieu; it is a hot evening, and hairdos are tumbling, perspiration is evident, and the viewer can almost smell the proceedings. (Ironically, much was made of the fact that the ball sequence featured a newly discovered waltz by Verdi.)

An international cast was superb, led by the trio of the French Alain Delon as the nephew, the Italian beauty Claudia Cardinale as his betrothed, and the American Burt Lancaster as the prince, brilliantly belying his early action-star image. *The Leopard* is a rarity, a drama less about war and the specific events of history than about the great social change of its time, and it succeeds triumphantly.

THE 20TH CENTURY

Many of the events of the twentieth century have been recorded on film as they happened, which has provided a wealth of background resource for re-creations of those events for dramas set against them. The major inspiration for the big movies about twentieth-century history has been revolution: the Russian, of course; the almost constant state of revolution in which China existed for the first half of the century; and, in Arabia, a strange subwar fought in the context of World War I in which the scattered tribes of Arabs used the greater conflict to gain help in a revolution against their Turkish overlords.

RUSSIA

The Russian Revolution was used as a backdrop for two large and spectacular films. *Doctor Zhivago* (1965) set the story of a sensitive doctor and his loves against the turbulence of the events that took place in Russia as it overthrew the czars and installed Bolshevism. Unfortunately, the personal drama was no match for the historical, and a game and talented cast was swallowed in a lengthy superproduction that at least always provides something to look at.

Nicholas and Alexandra (1971), on the other hand, took a real personal tragedy which was inextricably combined with the Revolution at the highest level, and made a riveting drama of it. The story of Czar Nicholas II (Michael Jayston), his German-born Czarina, Alexandra (Janet Suzman), and their five children (four beautiful daughters and one handsome, hemophiliac son) is as harrowing as that of Louis XVI and Marie Antoinette, replayed in a modern context. And as icing on the dramatic cake, there is the added factor of the sinister monk, Rasputin, whose healing power over the sickly heir to the throne led to a destructive power over the rulers of the country. This salmagundi of dramatic ingredients led to and was climaxed by the Russian Revolution, which in turn was of world-shaking importance not just because of its future but because it occurred in the middle of a World War and could have affected the outcome. *Nicholas and Alexandra* balanced the personal and historical drama expertly and served it up in a superbly mounted production, accurate to the smallest detail. Particularly notable are the two contrasting assassination scenes: that of Rasputin (Tom Baker—TV's Dr. Who), carried off by an effete aristocrat and his male lover in the middle of a lavish dinner

party, and which is suspensefully extended due to Rasputin's refusal to succumb to a series of lethal devices; and that of the royal family, shot as a group in the cellar of a small house in the distant reaches of Russia where they have been taken as prisoners.

ARABIA

The moribund Turkish Empire made the mistake of going into World War I on the side of Germany; to give the Turks a front within their own territory, Britain aided the tribes of Arabia in a bid for freedom. A legendary Britisher acted almost autonomously in uniting the tribes and organizing their struggle for independence. He was T. E. Lawrence, the subject of Lawrence of Arabia (1962), considered the greatest of modern superspectacles. It is indeed a colossal amalgam of spectacular battle scenes, endless sweeps of desert landscape (made for the wide screen), music of Tchaikovskian emotion, an appealing but ambiguous hero, and male rape (gingerly presented). It made a star of Peter O'Toole (Lawrence) as well as supporting player Omar Sharif, whose exotic, panethnic quality was to serve him well in many another historical movie. Too long for the limited attention span of modern audiences, it remains a model of epic filmmaking.

CHINA

The incredible history of China in the twentieth century has fascinated moviemakers and has been used as background in more than a few films, good, bad and indifferent. Three stand out for their size and quality. In the Boxer Rebel-

55 Days At Peking: An authentic Oriental extra eyes these three would-be Chinese with some misgiving. Nevertheless, Flora Robson as the Dowager Empress and Leo Genn (left) and Robert Helpmann as her two most powerful eunuchs did an excellent job of cross-racial acting.

Opposite:
The Good Earth: It seems as if half of California had been terraced into rice paddies for the stunning pastoral background of this epic of Chinese peasant life.

lion of 1903, a Chinese secret society—tacitly supported by what passed for a government—attempted to drive all foreigners from China. *55 Days at Peking* (1963) takes as its focus the beleaguered foreign compound in the Chinese capital, where representatives of the major nations and their families were attacked and besieged for fifty-five days before help arrived from the coast. The heroes are an American major (Charlton Heston) and the British consul (David Niven). Present to add glamour is a Russian countess (Ava Gardner) with a hot emerald necklace. There is a vivid re-creation of the intrigue-ridden Chinese court, dominated by the ancient Dowager Empress (Flora Robson, in yet another superb performance) and divided politically between two eunuchs (Leo Genn and the sinister Robert Helpmann). The suspense is terrific, the characters varied and fascinating, and there is one extraordinary set, the great gate to the Imperial City, the entire face of which suddenly opens like a Chinese box bristling with cannon.

One is never given the specific time or place of *The Good Earth* (1937); it is simply someplace in a timeless China where very little has changed in millennia. It must be simply assumed that it is this century, and the peasant family whose fortunes it follows are modern. But in it the small is made epic, and the trials of the family—locusts, famine, migration and unspecified turmoil (riot? revolution?) in the city where they go to seek sustenance—somehow achieve

The Good Earth: The peasant woman O-Lan (Luise Rainer, center at balustrade) gapes at the crowded city where her family has fled for food.

Opposite:

The Last Emperor: This gorgeously wrought spectacle reproduced the Forbidden City in the last days of the Manchu Empire by filming in, of all places, the Forbidden City.

the size of China itself. The central figure is the wife, whose totally passive persona is by some miracle the strength of the family. In this role, the Austrian Luise Rainer achieved a triumph (and an Oscar) by somehow negating herself and still dominating the screen. Paul Muni also gave a distinguished performance as the self-important husband, and the most impressive sequence, the plague of locusts that attacks the fields, is still an unparalleled screen effect.

The decline of the epic film in the last quarter of the twentieth century is due to many factors, not the least of them expense. The cost of the thousands of artisans and extras usually needed for such a project sent the locale of such filmmaking from America to Italy to Central Europe as expenses mounted in each place. Finally it seemed that there was no place in which such resources could be afforded, but in the 1980s there was still one—China. Italian director Bernardo Bertolucci joined forces with the Chinese government to make *The Last Emperor* (1987—nine Academy Awards), using the full resources of the government, which included supplying 19,000 extras. It is the biography of the last of the Manchu rulers of China, chosen as a child of three in 1908 by the Dowager Empress to succeed her. He was a puppet all his life: as a child ruled by the eunuchs of the court; as a figurehead when the Chinese Republic was established; as a playboy pawn of the Japanese, ruling the puppet empire of Manchukuo in occupied Manchuria; and as a brain-washed ordinary citizen of Communist China, where he became Henry Pu Yi, a gardener. This extraordinary story was brought to lavish life on the scene, and John Lone managed to make a real person of this sad, manipulated figure.

One can but wonder if the awards won by *The Last Emperor* were a response to seeing an authentic movie spectacle again, and one can but wonder if *The Last Emperor* might also be the last epic.

BIBLIOGRAPHY

Allan, Elkin, ed. *A Guide To World Cinema*. London: Whittet Books, Ltd., 1985.

Asimov, Isaac. *Asimov's Guide To the Bible*. New York: Avenel Books, 1981.

Bibby, Geoffrey. *Four Thousand Years Ago*. New York: Knopf, 1961.

Blum, Daniel. *Screen World: Vol. 8*. New York: Greenberg, 1957.

Cary, John. *Spectacular: The Story of Epic Films*. London: Castle, 1974.

Coe, Michael, Dean Snow, and Elizabeth Benson. *Atlas of Ancient America*. New York: Facts On File, 1986.

Deschner, Donald. *The Films of Cary Grant*. New York: Citadel, 1973.

Dickens, Homer. *The Films of Marlene Dietrich*. New York: Citadel, 1968.

Durant, Will. *The Age of Faith*. New York: Simon and Schuster, 1950.

————. *The Age of Reason Begins*. New York: Simon and Schuster, 1961.

————. *Caesar and Christ*. New York: Simon and Schuster, 1944.

————. *The Life of Greece*. New York: Simon and Schuster, 1939.

————. *Our Oriental Heritage*. New York: Simon and Schuster, 1935.

————. *The Reformation*. New York: Simon and Schuster, 1957.

Durant, Will, and Ariel Durant. *Rousseau and Revolution*. New York: Simon and Schuster, 1967.

————. *The Age of Napoleon*. New York: Simon and Schuster, 1975.

Eames, John Douglas. *The MGM Story*. New York: Simon and Schuster, 1976.

Foote, Shelby. *The Civil War, 3 vols*. New York: Random House, 1958.

Grun, Bernard. *The Timetables of History*. New York: Simon and Schuster, 1975.

Halliwell, Leslie. *The Filmgoer's Companion*. New York: Avon, 1978.

————. *Halliwell's Film and Video Guide*. New York: Scribner's, 1987.

Herold, J. Christopher. *The Age of Napoleon*. Boston: Houghton Mifflin, 1963.

Hibbert, Christopher. *The French Revolution*. New York: Penguin, 1982.

Kael, Pauline. *5001 Nights at the Movies*. New York: Holt, Rinehart and Winston, 1982.

————. *Hooked*. New York: E. P. Dutton, 1989.

Keller, Werner. *The Bible As History*. New York: William Morrow, 1981.

Maltin, Leonard. *TV Movies and Video Guide*. New York: New American Library, 1988.

Murray, Jane. *The Kings and Queens of England*. New York: Scribner's, 1974.

Pendle, George. *A History of Latin America*. London: Penguin, 1987 (rev.).

Renault, Mary. *The Nature of Alexander*. New York: Pantheon, 1975.

Ringold, Gene, and DeWitt Bodeen. *The Films of Cecil B. DeMille*. New York: Citadel, 1969.

Rogerson, John. *Atlas of the Bible*. New York: Facts On File, 1985.

Scherer, Margaret R. *The Legends of Troy in Art and Literature*. New York: Phaidon, 1963.

Slide, Anthony, and Edward Wagenknecht. *Fifty Great American Silent Films*. New York: Dover, 1980.

Steinberg, Cobbett. *Reel Facts*. New York: Vintage, 1978.

Taylor, Deems. *A Pictorial History of the Movies*. New York: Simon and Schuster, 1950.

Willis, John, ed. *Screen World: Vol. 17*. New York: Greenberg, 1966.

FILMOGRAPHY

Title	Year	With	Director	C or B/W
Abdication, The	1974	Peter Finch, Liv Ullmann	Anthony Harvey	C
Adventures of Marco Polo, The	1938	Gary Cooper, Sigrid Gurie	Archie Mayo	B/W
Adventures of Robin Hood, The	1938	Errol Flynn, Olivia de Havilland	Michael Curtiz / William Keighley	C
Agony and the Ecstacy, The	1965	Charlton Heston, Rex Harrison	Carol Reed	C
Alamo, The	1960	Richard Widmark, John Wayne	John Wayne	C
Alexander Nevsky	1938	Nikolai Cherkassov	Sergei Eisenstein	B/W
Alexander the Great	1956	Richard Burton, Fredric March	Robert Rossen	C
Alfred the Great	1969	David Hemmings, Michael York	Clive Donner	C
Anne of the Thousand Days	1969	Richard Burton, Geneviève Bujold	Charles Jarrott	C
Barabbas	1962	Anthony Quinn, Silvana Mangano	Richard Fleischer	C
Becket	1964	Richard Burton, Peter O'Toole	Peter Glenville	C
Ben-Hur	1926	Ramon Novarro, Francis X. Bushman	Fred Niblo	B/W
Ben Hur	1959	Charlton Heston, Stephen Boyd	William Wyler	C
Big Fisherman, The	1959	Howard Keel, Susan Kohner	Frank Borzage	C
Birth of a Nation, The	1915	Lillian Gish, Mae Marsh	D. W. Griffith	B/W
Bounty, The	1984	Mel Gibson, Anthony Hopkins	Roger Donaldson	C
Bride of Vengeance	1949	Paulette Goddard, John Lund	Mitchell Leisen	B/W
Brother Sun, Sister Moon	1973	Graham Faulkner, Judi Bowker	Franco Zeffirelli	C
Buccaneer, The	1938	Fredric March, Anthony Quinn	Cecil B. DeMille	B/W
Buccaneer, The	1958	Yul Brynner, Charlton Heston	Anthony Quinn	C
Caesar and Cleopatra	1946	Vivian Leigh, Claude Rains	Gabriel Pascal	C
Caligula	1980	Malcolm McDowell, Peter O'Toole	Tinto Brass	C
Captain from Castile	1947	Tyrone Power, Cesar Romero	Henry King	C
Catherine the Great	1934	Douglas Fairbanks, Jr., Elisabeth Bergner	Paul Czinner	B/W
Christopher Columbus	1949	Fredric March, Florence Eldridge	David Macdonald	C
Clan of the Cave Bear, The	1986	Daryl Hannah, Pamela Reed	Michael Chapman	C
Cleopatra	1917	Theda Bara	J. Gordon Edwards	B/W
Cleopatra	1934	Claudette Colbert, Warren William	Cecil B. DeMille	B/W
Cleopatra	1963	Elizabeth Taylor, Rex Harrison	Joseph L. Mankiewicz	C
Conqueror, The	1956	John Wayne, Susan Hayward	Dick Powell	C
Constantine and the Cross	1962	Cornel Wilde, Christine Kaufmann	Lionello de Felice	C
Cromwell	1970	Richard Harris, Alec Guinness	Ken Hughes	C
Crusades, The	1935	Loretta Young, Henry Wilcoxon	Cecil B. DeMille	B/W
David and Bathsheba	1951	Gregory Peck, Susan Hayward	Henry King	C
Demetrius and the Gladiators	1954	Victor Mature, Susan Hayward	Delmer Daves	C
Desirée	1954	Jean Simmons, Marlon Brando	Henry Koster	C
Diane	1956	Lana Turner, Roger Moore	David Miller	C

Title	Year	With	Director	C or B/W
Doctor Zhivago	1965	Omar Sharif, Julie Christie	David Lean	C
Drums Along the Mohawk	1939	Claudette Colbert, Henry Fonda	John Ford	C
Duel in the Sun	1946	Jennifer Jones, Gregory Peck	King Vidor	C
Egyptian, The	1954	Jean Simmons, Edmund Purdom	Michael Curtiz	C
El Cid	1961	Charlton Heston, Sophia Loren	Anthony Mann	C
Esther and the King	1960	Joan Collins, Richard Egan	Raoul Walsh	C
Fabiola	1947	Michele Morgan, Henri Vidal	Alessandro Blasetti	B/W
Fall of the Roman Empire, The	1964	Sophia Loren, Stephen Boyd	Anthony Mann	C
55 Days at Peking	1963	Charlton Heston, Ava Gardner	Nicholas Ray	C
Forever Amber	1947	Linda Darnell, Cornel Wilde	Otto Preminger	C
Genghis Khan	1965	Omar Sharif, Stephen Boyd	Henry Levin	C
Gone With the Wind	1939	Vivien Leigh, Clark Gable	Victor Fleming	C
Good Earth, The	1937	Paul Muni, Luise Rainer	Sidney Franklin	B/W
Gospel According to St. Matthew, The	1966	Enrique Irazoqui, Susanna Pasolini	Pier Paolo Pasolini	B/W
Greatest Story Ever Told, The	1965	Max Von Sydow, Charlton Heston	George Stevens	C
Hannibal	1960	Victor Mature, Rita Gam	Edgar G. Ulmer	C
Helen of Troy	1955	Rossana Podesta, Jacques Sernas	Robert Wise	C
Henry V	1944	Laurence Olivier, Robert Newton	Laurence Olivier	C
Henry V	1989	Kenneth Branagh, Paul Scofield	Kenneth Branagh	C
Howards of Virginia, The	1940	Cary Grant, Martha Scott	Frank Lloyd	B/W
Hunchback of Notre Dame, The	1923	Lon Chaney, Patsy Ruth Miller	Wallace Worsley	B/W
Hunchback of Notre Dame, The	1939	Charles Laughton, Maureen O'Hara	William Dieterle	B/W
I, Claudius	1937	Charles Laughton, Flora Robson	Josef von Sternberg	B/W
Intolerance	1916	Lillian Gish, Mae Marsh	D. W. Griffith	B/W
Iron Horse, The	1924	George O'Brien, Madge Bellamy	John Ford	B/W
Ivan the Terrible (Ivan Groznyi) I	1943	Nikolai Cherkassov, Ludmilla Tselikovskaya	Sergei Eisenstein	B/W
Ivan the Terrible (Ivan Groznyi) II	1946	Nikolai Cherkassov, Serafima Birman	Sergei Eisenstein	B/W
Ivanhoe	1952	Elizabeth Taylor, Robert Taylor	Richard Thorpe	C
Joan of Arc	1948	Ingrid Bergman, Jose Ferrer	Victor Fleming	C
Joan the Woman	1917	Geraldine Farrar, Raymond Hatton	Cecil B. DeMille	B/W
John Paul Jones	1959	Robert Stack, Charles Coburn	John Farrow	C
Juarez	1939	Paul Muni, Bette Davis	William Dieterle	B/W
Julius Caesar	1953	Marlon Brando, James Mason	Joseph L. Mankiewicz	B/W
Jupiter's Darling	1955	Esther Williams, Howard Keel	George Sidney	C
King David	1985	Richard Gere, Edward Woodward	Bruce Beresford	C
King of Kings	1927	H. B. Warner, Dorothy Cumming	Cecil B. DeMille	B/W
King of Kings	1961	Jeffrey Hunter, Siobhan McKenna	Nicholas Ray	C
Kings of the Sun	1963	Yul Brynner, George Chakiris	J. Lee-Thompson	C
Knights of the Round Table	1953	Robert Taylor, Ava Gardner	Richard Thorpe	C
Lady Jane	1985	Helena Bonham Carter, Cary Elwes	Trevor Nunn	C
Last Days of Pompeii, The	1935	Preston Foster, Basil Rathbone	Ernest B. Schoedsack	B/W
Last Emperor, The	1987	John Lone, Peter O'Toole	Bernardo Bertolucci	C
Last Temptation of Christ, The	1988	Willem Dafoe, Barbara Hershey	Martin Scorsese	C
Last Valley, The	1971	Omar Sharif, Michael Caine	James Clavell	C
Lawrence of Arabia	1962	Peter O'Toole, Alec Guinness	David Lean	C
Leopard, The	1963	Burt Lancaster, Alain Delon	Luchino Visconti	C
Lion in Winter, The	1968	Peter O'Toole, Katharine Hepburn	Anthony Harvey	C
Madame Dubarry	1931	Dolores Del Rio, Reginald Owen	William Dieterle	B/W
Man for All Seasons, A	1966	Paul Scofield, Wendy Hiller	Fred Zinnemann	C
Marie Antoinette	1938	Norma Shearer, Tyrone Power	W. S. Van Dyke	B/W
Marseillaise, La	1938	Pierre Renoir, Louis Jouvet	Jean Renoir	B/W
Mary of Scotland	1936	Katharine Hepburn, Fredric March	John Ford	B/W
Mary, Queen of Scots	1971	Vanessa Redgrave, Glenda Jackson	Charles Jarrott	C
Mutiny on the Bounty	1935	Clark Gable, Charles Laughton	Frank Lloyd	B/W
Mutiny on the Bounty	1962	Marlon Brando, Trevor Howard	Lewis Milestone	C
Napoleon	1927	Albert Dieudonné, Gina Manes	Abel Gance	B/W
Nicholas and Alexandra	1971	Michael Jayston, Janet Suzman	Franklin Schaffner	C
Northwest Mounted Police	1940	Gary Cooper, Madeleine Carroll	Cecil B. DeMille	C
Northwest Passage	1940	Spencer Tracy, Robert Young	King Vidor	C
Omar Khayyam	1957	Cornel Wilde, Debra Paget	William Dieterle	C
Orphans of the Storm	1922	Lillian Gish, Dorothy Gish	D. W. Griffith	B/W
Plymouth Adventure	1952	Spencer Tracy, Gene Tierney	Clarence Brown	C
Pride and the Passion, The	1957	Cary Grant, Frank Sinatra	Stanley Kramer	C
Prince of Foxes	1949	Tyrone Power, Orson Welles	Henry King	B/W
Private Life of Henry VIII, The	1933	Charles Laughton, Elsa Lanchester	Alexander Korda	B/W
Private Lives of Elizabeth and Essex, The	1939	Bette Davis, Errol Flynn	Michael Curtiz	C
Prodigal, The	1955	Lana Turner, Edmund Purdom	Richard Thorpe	C
Queen Christina	1933	Greta Garbo, John Gilbert	Rouben Mamoulian	B/W
Queen Elizabeth (La Reine Elizabeth)	1912	Sarah Bernhardt	Henri Desfontaines	B/W
Queen of Babylon, The	1956	Rhonda Fleming, Ricardo Montalban	Carlo Bragaglia	C
Queen of Sheba	1921	Betty Blythe, Fritz Leiber	J. Gordon Edwards	B/W
Quentin Durward	1955	Robert Taylor, Kay Kendall	Richard Thorpe	C

Title	Year	With	Director	C or B/W
Quest For Fire	1981	Ron Perlman, Rae Dawn Chong	Jean-Jacques Annaud	C
Quo Vadis	1951	Robert Taylor, Deborah Kerr	Mervyn LeRoy	C
Revolution	1985	Al Pacino, Donald Sutherland	Hugh Hudson	C
Robe, The	1953	Jean Simmons, Richard Burton	Henry Koster	C
Robin Hood	1922	Douglas Fairbanks, Wallace Beery	Allan Dwan	B/W
Royal Hunt of the Sun	1969	Robert Shaw, Christopher Plummer	Irving Lerner	C
Royal Scandal, A	1945	Tallulah Bankhead, Charles Coburn	Ernst Lubitsch, Otto Preminger	B/W
Salome	1918	Theda Bara	J. Gordon Edwards	B/W
Salomé	1923	Nazimova	Charles Bryant	B/W
Salome	1953	Rita Hayworth, Stewart Granger	William Dieterle	C
Samson and Delilah	1949	Victor Mature, Hedy Lamarr	Cecil B. DeMille	C
Saraband for Dead Lovers	1948	Stewart Granger, Joan Greenwood	Basil Dearden	C
Scarlet Empress, The	1934	Marlene Dietrich, John Lodge	Josef von Sternberg	B/W
Seven Cities of Gold	1955	Richard Egan, Anthony Quinn	Robert D. Webb	C
Sign of the Cross, The	1932	Fredric March, Claudette Colbert	Cecil B. DeMille	B/W
Sign of the Pagan	1954	Jack Palance, Jeff Chandler	Douglas Sirk	C
Silver Chalice, The	1954	Paul Newman, Virginia Mayo	Victor Saville	C
Sodom and Gomorrah	1962	Stewart Granger, Pier Angeli	Robert Aldrich	C
Solomon and Sheba	1959	Yul Brynner, Gina Lollobrigida	King Vidor	C
Spartacus	1960	Kirk Douglas, Jean Simmons	Stanley Kubrick	C
Sword and the Rose, The	1953	Richard Todd, Glynis Johns	Ken Annakin	C
Ten Commandments, The	1923	Theodore Roberts, Charles de Roche	Cecil B. DeMille	B/W
Ten Commandments, The	1956	Charlton Heston, Yul Brynner	Cecil B. DeMille	C
300 Spartans, The	1962	Richard Egan, Diane Baker	Rudolph Mate	C
Three Musketeers, The	1921	Douglas Fairbanks, Barbara La Marr	Fred Niblo	B/W
Three Musketeers, The	1948	Gene Kelly, Lana Turner	George Sidney	C
Three Musketeers, The	1973	Michael York, Faye Dunaway	Richard Lester	C
Trojan Women, The	1972	Vanessa Redgrave, Katharine Hepburn	Michael Cacoyannis	C
Unconquered	1947	Gary Cooper, Paulette Goddard	Cecil B. DeMille	C
Union Pacific	1939	Barbara Stanwyck, Joel McCrea	Cecil B. DeMille	B/W
Vikings, The	1958	Kirk Douglas, Tony Curtis	Richard Fleischer	C
Virgin Queen, The	1955	Bette Davis, Richard Todd	Henry Koster	C
Walk with Love and Death, A	1969	Anjelica Huston, Assaf Dayan	John Huston	C
War and Peace	1956	Audrey Hepburn, Henry Fonda	King Vidor	C
War and Peace (Voina I Mir)	1963 –67	Ludmila Savelyeva, Sergei Bondarchuk	Sergei Bondarchuk	C
Waterloo	1970	Rod Steiger, Christopher Plummer	Sergei Bondarchuk	C
Young Bess	1953	Jean Simmons, Charles Laughton	George Sidney	C
Zulu	1964	Stanley Baker, Michael Caine	Cy Endfield	C

INDEX

All references are to page numbers; numbers in *italic* type refer to pages on which illustrations appear.

Abdication, The, 163
Abel, Walter, 151
Abram, 11
Absolom, 23
Addams, Dawn, 156
Adventures of Marco Polo, The, 112; *111, 112*
Adventures of Robin Hood, The, 102, 104; *103*
Agony and the Ecstacy, The, 128; *128, 129*
Agrippina, 67
Ahasuerus, 32; *32*
    see also Xerxes I
Aherne, Brian, 217; *216*
Aimée, Anouk, 11
Akhenaton, 12, 13
Alamo, The, 207
Alden, John, 153, 156
Alexander I of Russia, 182
Alexander VI, Pope, 123
Alexander the Great, 35, 36, 48
Alexander the Great, 34, 35–36; *34*
Alexander Nevsky, 109–10, 148; *109*
Alexandra, Czarina, 220
Alfred, King of Saxony, 89, 90
Alfred, The Great, 90; *90, 91*
Allyson, June, 151
American Revolution, 167
    Howards of Virginia, The, 172, 175; *174*
    John Paul Jones, 175, 176; *175, 176*
    Revolution, 175–76; *177*
Amnon, 23
Anderson, Judith, 20, 57, 141
Anderson, Maxwell, 116, 134
Anderson, Michael, Jr., 53
Andromache, 22
Angeli, Pier, 12, 72, 76; *73*
Anjou, Count of, 99
Anne of Austria, 151

Anne of Cleves, 130
Anne of England, 156
Anne of the Thousand Days, 132, 134; *133*
Anouilh, Jean, 99, 100
Antony, Marc, 39, 42, 44, 49, 104
Armendariz, Pedro, 147; *147*
Arthur, King, 87
Artos, 83
Aslan, Gregoire, 50; *50*
Atahualpa, 128, 130
Attila, 81, 83
Auel, Jean M., 10
Aurelius, Marcus, 78, 79
Aylmer, Felix, 87, 105, 115, 126; *87*

Baker, Stanley, 218
Baker, Tom, 220
Baketamon, 12
Bankhead, Tallulah, 166; *166*
Bara, Theda, 9, 42, 57, 114; *8*
Barabbas, 49, 58
Barabbas, 58; *59*
Barbier, George, 112; *112*
Barnes, Binnie, 132
Barrett, Wilson, 70
Barrie, Wendy, 131, 132; *131*
Barry, John, 100
Barrymore, John, 183, 186; *186*
Barrymore, Lionel, 212
Bathsheba, 23, 25, 27, 28
Baxter, Anne, 18, 167
Bazlen, Brigid, 50; *50*
Beardsley, Aubrey, 57
Beauharnais, Josephine de, 192
Beauve, St., 192
Becket (movie), 96, 99–100, 105; *97, 98, 99*

Becket (stage play), 99
Becket, Thomas, 99, 100
Beery, Wallace, 104
Bellamy, Madge, 212
Bel-shar-utsur, 28
Belshazzar, King, 28
Ben-Hur (1926), 61, 64; *60, 61*
Ben Hur (1959), 61, 62, 63, 64, 79; *61, 62–63*
Bera, Queen, 11
Berengaria of Navarre, 100, 102, 104
Bergman, Ingrid, 116, 119; *117*
Bergner, Elisabeth, 164; *164*
Bernhardt, Sarah, 138; *138*
Bertolucci, Bernardo, 228
Bettis, Valerie, 57
Big Fisherman, The, 58; *58*
Billy Budd, 179
Birth of a Nation, The, 203, 207–8; *206, 207*
Bligh, William, 176, 179, 182
Bloom, Claire, 36, 205
Blythe, Betty, 23, 25; *23*
Boelyn, Anne, 130, 134, 137
Bonaparte, Napoleon, 182, 192, 193, 194, 195, 198, 201
Bond, Ward, 172; *173*
Bondarchuk, Sergei, 200, 201
Borgia, Cesare, 123, 126
Borgia, Lucrezia, 123, 126
Borgnine, Ernest, 89
Bothwell, Earl of, 141, 145
Bounty, The, 182, 184; *184, 185*
Bowie, Jim, 207
Bowker, Judi, 110
Boxer Rebellion, 225–26
    55 Days In Peking, 226; *226*
Boyd, Stephen, 62, 64, 78, 79, 107; *62–63, 78*
Bradford, William, 156
Branagh, Kenneth, 116; *116*
Brando, Marlon, 46, 182, 184, 194; *46, 185, 194*
Brandon, Charles, 132
Bride of Vengeance, 123, 126; *124*
Brother Sun, Sister Moon, 110; *110*

236

CREDITS